Entheogens, Myth & Human Consciousness

by Carl A. P. Ruck
Mark A. Hoffman

RONIN

Books-for-Independent-Minds

Berkeley, California
www.roninpub.com

Another **RONIN** Book by Carl Ruck
Sacred M ushrooms of the Goddess
Secrets of Eleusis

Entheogens, Myth & Human Consciousness

by Carl A. P. Ruck
Mark A. Hoffman

Entheogens, Myth & Human Consciousness
Copyright 2013 by Carl A. P. Ruck &
Mark A Hoffman, ISBN : 9781579511418

Published by
Ronin Publishing, Inc.
PO Box 3436
Oakland, CA 94609
www.roninpub.com

Editor: Mark Estren
Cover & Interior Design:Beverly Potter
Cover Painting: Woliul Hasau Unsplash
Fonts: Goudy, Papyrus, Herculanum, Navel

Library of Congress Card Number: 20129480279
Distributed to the book trade by Publishers Group West

TABLE OF CONTENTS

First Clinical LSD Experience
(Influenced by Strobe Light)

My consciousness expanded at an in-
conceivable speed and reached cosmic
dimensions. There was no more difference between me and the universe. While
this was happening, I found myself at the
center of a cosmic drama of unimaginable
dimensions. I would say today that I pos-
sibly experienced the big bang, passage
through black holes and white holes,
identification with exploding super novas
and collapsing stars, and other strange
phenomena.

—Stanislav Grof
The Potential of Entheogens
as Catalysts of Spiritual Development

Astrologers by Robert Fludd

PREFACE

This is a dangerous book. If you wish to experience an awakening, be warned: this book has no railings. You will never see the World the same way. Your eyes will be forever opened and everything you have been taught about Religion will be understood as "cowardly evasions" at best. You will never be able to be fooled again. Hereafter it will be your choice to be fooled. The universal reflex to keep the eyes shut in a time of fear will no longer be an option.

Great teachings emphasize that all knowledge must come from the quest for the truth. No matter what the consequences, the truth must be told. The truth does hurt, and this one will leave a mark—like a child who stood in the midst of a most beautiful forest and upon return later in life sees that a vast city now stands in its place. Like the child, the viewer/reader will be perplexed. The scar is upon the heart and the loss of Eden will never go away. The enlightened adult can forgive, but the child within will remember.

We will not have to wait long to see consequences from this work, because the speed of the Internet is in place. The shock wave from this book will travel like a tsunami and will wash upon every shore where false temples have been built. The astounding collection of knowledge in these chapters contains the parallel impact of the revelation in Cosmology, that we see only one percent of what we call the Universe. Ninety-nine percent is invisible to us. The cosmological conundrum mirrors the metaphysical crisis of belief.

The daunting hunt of our Species will continue even after all the temples are gone. As with the concept of Zero ... nothing does matter. The Enigma is the energy of this book. The Query is "God." The Walkabout is the journey to the rim of the abyss. Only the courageous will embark on such a dangerous quest.

So be it. Our being was made flesh to take on such a task. This guide, like Saint Michael's Sword, certainly improves our chances.

—Rev. Richard Emmanuel
Pastor of the Theosophist Church
East Gloucester, Massachusetts

foreword

Dangerous Knowledge

The remains of John Wycliffe were exhumed in the year 1428, burned, and cast into the River Swift, a tributary of the Avon in central England, along with all his books. He had been Master of Balliol College, but was declared a heretic at the Ecumenical Council of Constance in 1415. His crime was that he had translated the Bible into English. The translation of Scripture by unlicensed laity was punishable by charges of heresy since it opened the floodgate of undisciplined exegesis.

The Second Vatican Council opened with intense optimism under Pope John XXIII in 1962 and closed under his successor Paul VI in 1965. This was the great liberalizing reexamination of dogma that accepted the Mass conducted in the vernacular. As part of this liberal movement, the vast documents of the Vatican Library were made accessible to young seminarians around the world. The doors closed with the ascension of Paul VI. Many student theologians deserted the Church, and even in so profoundly a Catholic nation as Ireland, there is now a great paucity of new young priests to replace the generation of Vatican II who now are reaching the age of retirement.

Knowledge is dangerous. It both jeopardizes the familiar establishment, even though it might be in error, and reveals long-suppressed secrets that encourage irresponsible innovation. Vatican II coincided with the realization of the role that visionary sacraments have played in the emergence of human consciousness and

Lightning bolt penetrating the spread vulva of the volcano, contemporary painting making the sexual metaphor explicit

the relationship of mankind to spiritual dimensions. This offered new perspectives on the genesis of Christianity and on the marketplace of novel religions originating in the New World in the 19th and 20th centuries. The door that had opened was quickly posted with a placard announcing no admittance in the ensuing conservative papacies. The short glimpse into the mystical and hermetic tradition of Christianity left many young people perplexed and without guidance

The Cave

Myth is a reflex of psychoactive sacraments—entheo-gens—going back in history to the Paleolithic Age, and these same myths serve as a guide for future spiritual development. The fundamental metaphor is the Cave, which has multiple referents of any enclosed space, from natural subterranean chambers and their connota-tions of the womb to architectural simu-lacra as temples and religious sanctuar-ies, from which the initiate experiences transcendence to the rim of the cosmos, known as the fiery realm of the empyrean.

Knowledge jeopardizes the familiar establishment, even though it might be in error, and reveals long-sup-pressed secrets that encour-age irresponsible innovation.

The prototypical Cave is the volcano, in whose forge the soul is transmuted from base metal to celestial gold. A pillar of fire like a bolt of lightning transfixes the sacred mountain, providing a pathway uniting the alchemical caldera with the universe. The spiritual flight that opens the heavens has been at the origin of religions and has served as well for the inauguration of recent homebred adaptations of ancient mysteries in the New World.

Although all mythologies tell the same story, the traditions of Europe that derive from the Classical world and Judeo-Christianity were declared off limits for those seeking guidance for a tour of the empyrean. This was unfortunate, since Classical myth presents some of the most perfect exemplars of human experience and has served to delineate basic psychological paradigms.

In this guide we will correct the error by demonstrating the centrality of psychoactive sacraments to the evolution of the Western World. In the pages that follow, we will provide a historical perspective on the role of entheogens in the evolution of human consciousness, and a guide for those perplexed about both the dangers of their abuse and their potential for cognitive transcendence.

1

ꝳYTH OF ꞓCSTASY

The worldwide myth about how fire was stolen from the heavens reflects humankind's first conscious awareness of its relationship to the divine. Fire is metaphoric for the semen of deity and is found in the psychoactive plants that figure in the primordial rituals of shamanism that established the plant as a metaphoric tree affording a pathway of transcendence. A flaming pillar extends from the fiery surround of the cosmos through the sacred mountain to the volcanic crucible in the netherworld. The dietary restrictions of an ancient Christian heretical sect that continued into recent times reflect this myth of ecstasy.

Man at first did not have fire. It was hidden away, deep in the earth, far in the sky. Many are the stories of the thieving tricksters who stole it, rebellious angels, culture heroes, shape-shifters, shamanic familiars, coyote, rabbit, beaver, pigeon, crow, and even grandmother spider. They stole it either from the highest heavens beyond the sun or from the fiery crucible beneath the volcano, and they gave it as a great boon to mankind. These thieves were at the

And Azazel taught men metallurgy, the metals of the earth and how to work them, and metallic distillates. And his fallen angels copulated with humans and taught enchantments, root-cuttings, astrology.

—*Book of Enoch*

Thou, O Agni, art highest vital power, the life- and death-bestowing Fire, the treasure found far away in the highest firmament, deeply hidden in the earth. The hero who knows brought you back from where you were hidden from mankind.

—*Rig Veda*

very beginning of our species; and we humans were creatures that the trickster fashioned, often out of clay, hardened to durability in the volcanic forge like a potter's vessel, to contain the burning gift. The theft of fire and the making of the first humans are interchangeable themes, synchronous events in the evolution of our species. Fire was at the origin of man's superiority, when humans first noticed their nakedness, the primordial sign of their awakening consciousness, and thus rose above the other beasts.

With fire came also enchantments, charms, witchcraft, the art of cutting medicinal and magical roots, the gathering of drug plants, herbs, metallurgy, ecstasy, all knowledge. Fire was Light, spiritual Illumination. With fire, the creatures of clay might dare encroach upon the realms of the gods, who jealously had hidden it away for themselves. The thieves who stole it were labeled as enemies, cast from the heavens into eternal torment for revealing the secrets of the gods. In Judeo-Christianity, the fire-thief was Azazel, who was also called Lucifer, the 'Bearer of the Light,' the brightest of the angels, condemned for the theft and identified as Satan.

The fire became like a pillar of light, a flaming column, and a shining pathway for transcendent flight right through the molten core of the mountain back to the zenith of the cosmos. Before man learned to master it with the fire-stick, the two naturally available sources of fire would have been the erupting mountain and the fall of the lightning bolt, the dual termini of the pathway. It was the seminal flux of the heavens penetrating the vulva of Gaia, the Earth, the fiery potion caught in the chalice of clay that was a human. It was the copulation with angels. The fire of the intellect, the spirit of the soul, was mankind's portion of divinity.

Plants of Illumination

The most famous of these tricksters was the Greek titan Prometheus. The same themes, however, can be traced in mythologies worldwide. The theft of fire is a mythical motif analogous to the theft of a magical plant whose spiritual persona is quintessential fire. Among the Huichol Indians of the Sierra Madre Occidental of northern Mexico, it is the great ancestral shaman Tatewari, named as 'Grandfather Fire,' who still leads the three hundred mile initiatory pilgrimage of the vision quest to gather the sacred peyote. In performing the arduous trek, those participating in the hunt are repeating the original mythic quest for the sacred plant.

In Vedic tradition, Agni, the god of the sacred fire, found the intoxicating Soma plant in the highest firmament, but also in the deepest recess of the Earth. Agni is the first word of the Vedas, perhaps the first word ever written. He represents the

Apollo in the Forge of Vulcan

I hunted fire, stolen, stuffed in a reed cage for botanical drugs and medicines, herbs of ecstasy, the fount that taught humans all they know, how to cope with every need.

—Aeschylus
Prometheus

cause of all change, the metabolism of the cosmos, the guiding Light.

In Greek mythology, the titans were the children of Gaia, the race before the Olympian gods. Prometheus's theft of fire is analogous to acquiring access to the magical food of the gods, the food that made them divine. Metaphorically, it was called nectar and ambrosia, but it was found as the fiery spirit resident in special plants and botanical potions whose intoxicating properties were the vehicle for human transcendence along the axis of the flaming pillar. Prometheus is often a thematic double for Hephaestus, who is called Vulcan in Latin. Both Hephaestus and Vulcan are named for the 'volcano,' whose forge they tend as blacksmiths. Prometheus is named as the 'one who knows.' The fire-thief and the volcanic forge are associated in mythologies around the world, along with the goblin henchmen who assist them in their metallurgy.

The Greek traditions are one of the best-preserved mythologies, documented in extensive literature and art for over two and a half millennia. The motif of the stolen fire as a plant of ecstasy is explicit in the earliest accounts. We are told that Prometheus stole fire hidden in the special container that herbalists use to gather their botanical specimens. In Greek, it was named the narthex, traditionally made of a hollow reed. In it were placed magical herbs, potent roots, dug and cut, like hidden treasure, alchemical gold, the same knowledge that Azazel taught. The narthex etymologically designates a 'repository for narcotics,' a *narco-thex*. In retaliation for his gift to humankind, Zeus chained Prometheus to a volcano. An eagle gnaws eternally at his liver, the organ of the body that filters toxins. It was considered the seat of divine perception and clairvoyance because it mirrored exactly the shape of the cosmos.

Forbidden Fruit

These plants of ecstasy worldwide are metaphorically the forbidden fruit of a special tree. Many are the tales also of this forbidden fruit. Most famous are Yahweh's Tree in Eden, and the Nordic *Yggdrasil*, for which Odin sacrificed an eye. Like the Vedic *Kalpavriksha*, the Tree satisfied a hunger for every need. Like the Nordic apples of Idunn, it offered a food of immortality.

In Greek myth, the tree grew in the Garden of the Western Sisterhood, called the Hesperides. It was located topographically at the straits of Gibraltar. Many heroes confronted the serpent guarding the Tree. When Hercules took on the task, Prometheus told him not to enter the garden himself. Instead, he was to send Atlas, who was Prometheus's brother in the West, into the garden. Prometheus chained to the volcano in the east and Atlas as the pillar forced to hold aloft the

Perseus with harvested head
of the Medusa.

heavens in the West are complementary figures. The high Atlas Mountains, which the titan personifies, show evidence of massive volcanic eruptions; and in the eastern Caucasus Mountains, Mt. Elbrus, which is now dormant, was once one of the world's most active volcanoes. These mountain ranges were the limits of the Mediterranean world.

Odin holding a shamanic drinking goblet while seated on his Sleipnir

Jason and his fellow Argonauts, the sailors of the ship Argo, found the Tree instead in the Far East, where Prometheus was tormented for his theft of fire. There its fruit was described as a Golden Fleece, but it was recognized even in antiquity that the word for 'fleece' and 'apple' was homonymous. Both fleece and apple are merely metaphors for the psychoactive fruit.

The hero Perseus was the first to visit the Garden of the Hesperides, and he picked the fruit of the Tree with a harvesting knife as a mushroom, metaphorically anthropomorphized as the head of the Gorgon Medusa.

Jason and his crew also visited the Western Garden the day after Hercules passed through, and the guardian serpent's tail was still writhing, attracting flies that withered and died in its festering wounds. Flies do not die in rotting flesh. The particular species of the mushroom involved in all these

The horse is also a motif in these myths since the fruit affords the hero a marvelous steed for his heroic flight.

mythological accounts, including the Tree in Eden, was the *Amanita muscaria*, commonly called the fly-agaric, for its attractiveness to flies that seem to wither and die in its juice. The prototypic exemplar of all the drug plants and golden apples of Illumination was a magically sacred mushroom.

When Perseus severed the neck of the Gorgon Medusa, the flying horse Pegasus emerged. The horse is also a motif in these myths since the fruit affords the hero a marvelous steed for his heroic flight. Pegasus is named for the "fountain" of inspiring waters that flowed from his hooves. *Yggdrasil* means Odin's horse, who was the eight-legged Sleipnir. He is depicted riding Sleipnir holding a shamanic goblet. The fruit of the forbidden tree was the food of ecstasy.

That this shamanic food was indeed a mushroom is made even more explicit in the Greek rituals of herb gatherers. The Mushroom itself, in fact, was the Tree. The narthex or narcotic container was also called the *thyrsus*. It was the emblem of Bacchus, the god of ecstasy and intoxication. In common culinary terminology, the stipe

Dante's View of the Universe

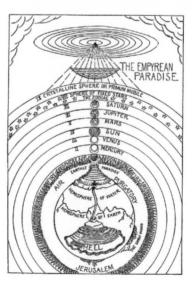

The Empyrean, seen as the opposite of Hell, extending through the circular (volcanic) holy mount of Jerusalem,.

or 'trunk' of the mushroom Tree was called a *thyrsus* in Latin, with its psychoactive cap spreading above like twigs stuffed into the narthex container. It fruited when a bolt of lightning transfixed the pathway from the celestial highest to the chthonic depths, bursting suddenly upward exactly where the bolt had fallen.

In the volcanic forge the blacksmith employs the thunder hammer as his implement. Numerous sacred replicas of these thunder hammers, worn as jewelry, resemble mushroom caps. Thor himself is depicted as a fungal anthropomorphism in a 9th century statuette from Iceland.

2

SEMEN FROM THE HEAVENS

The Tree of the Western Sisterhood, with the Gorgon head as its fruiting apple, first sprouted at the spot where the sun goes down, and the narrow Straits of Gibraltar suggest a gateway to a world beyond. There, Zeus consummated his wedding to Hera with a lightning bolt molded in the volcanic forge and plunged into her receptive vulva. Thus the upper and lower realms were joined along the fiery pathway, the volcanic vulva of Gaia or earth in the persona of Hera with the inseminating fire of the cosmos. Semen, fire, and the plant of divinity are analogous metaphors, as is also the blood of the menstrual flux. Semen is fire in water. The metallurgist who fashioned the molten bolt was Hera's own son, the lord of the volcano, Hephaestus/Vulcan. It was he who chained Prometheus to the mountain.

> The intellect is aflame. Ideas are aflame. Consciousness at the intellect is aflame.
>
> —Fire Sermon of the Buddha

In Ovid's playful account of Zeus's courting of Semele—*Metamorphoses 3*, the mother of Bacchus/Dionysus, makes it clear that Zeus always mated with his wife via the thunderbolt forged in the volcano by the smith and his henchmen with the thunder hammer.

The sexual metaphor of fire is implicit in the tale of its theft. It glows at the tip of the narthex reed, like the exposed blood-suffused *glans* of the erect penis. Traditionally, this is how fire was borrowed, carried from one place to another in the smoldering matrix. In some tales, it is the fire-stick that is stolen, making the sexual innuendo even more explicit. This is the stick that is drilled and twirled in a receptive hole to generate fire by friction. It was only this trick that made fire truly accessible. *Fomes fomentarius* fungus is highly flammable and was used at least as early as the Neolithic period as kindling for the fire.

Commonly called hoof fungus, this shelf fungus looks like the hoof of a giant horse when attached to the trunk of the tree, suggesting the metaphor of the magical steed and the stairway to heaven, like Odin's tree-horse *Yggdrasil* or the flying Pegasus. Interestingly it is often found on birch trees which also host the psychoactive Amanita red mushroom as the golden fruit at its base. Metaphoric names for the mushroom abound, identifying it as either the penetrating penis or the receptive vulva. The highly flammable tinder mushroom was indispensable to early man for making fire, and mushroom names often elaborate the motif of sex and love. The word 'spark' belongs to this linguistic cluster. The word itself derives ultimately from the metaphor of the sponge that yields fungus in Latin.

Sparks Fly Upward

Fire is both the heat perceptible in living creatures and the clear transmutation of matter as it dissipates into the fumes of spiritual transcendence. It is the mediator between gods and men. The burning of sacrificial offerings ritually enacts this significance of fire, returning the inedible portion of the victim to the skies.

The ancients believed the empyrean to be the abode of God and the angels; a realm of pure fire or light in the highest reaches of heaven—paradise.

Prometheus, the fire thief, taught man the trick of sacrificial fire. So, too, did Loki, the Norse trickster who was god of fire, and the father of Odin's Sleipnir. Loki stole the apples of Idunn, making clear the analogous motifs of fire and shamanic plants. Prometheus played his trick with the sacrificial offering at a settlement called Opium-town. In cremation, the corporal body was thought to dissolve back into plants and water, while the spirit ascended with the flames.

Fire is cognate with consciousness, intelligence, the *scintilla animae* or "spark of the soul". As one of the four elements, it alone has no substance, no material exis-tence. Fire leaps upward from any source, even the vol-canic forge. It must go on in that ascending flight forever until it reaches the farthest limit of the cosmos. There it collects, forming the fiery surround of the entire universe. That outer limit is the empyrean, the conglomerate of every fire ever lit, every mind that ever lived.

If there are beings that inhabit the empyreal realm, they are anthro-pomorphized as creatures so pure

Ether is another name for this mythological realm.

that they are composed solely of ethereal light. Ether is another name for this mythological realm. In computer technology, the term has been updated as Ethernet.

Isis Speaks

In Euripides' *Helen* tragedy, the clairvoyant priestess called "God-Perception" or Theonoë merged her mind

with this network of cosmic consciousness, which is
higher even than the gods themselves. This source of
inspired knowledge allows her to act while the gods are
locked in bitter debate. She is free to choose an ethical
principle beyond their selfish bickering. So, too, did the
medieval German mystic Meister Eckhart posit a Godhead beyond God, for which he was tried as a heretic.

Set in Egypt, *Helen* tells the tale in which the beautiful woman who caused the Trojan War actually never
went to Troy. It was only a hallucinatory image that the
warriors fought over in the disastrous war. Meanwhile,
the real Helen is a faithful wife of her absent husband
Menelaus who determinedly fends off sexual attacks
at home in Egypt. The scenario involves confusing
appearances where things are never what they seem.
The priestess Theonoë must have been costumed as an
Egyptian, probably resembling Isis.

Euripides' play was the first fantasy in the Egyptian
Mysteries. Mozart's *Magic Flute* belongs to this tradition. Euripides was condemned by fellow Freemasons
for revealing their secrets of the goddess Isis. In the
stage setting designed by the Prussian architect Shin-
kel, a screen depicting an Egyptian temple implausibly
lodged within a Cave is raised to reveal the humorously
obscure and incomprehensible Queen of the Night,
singing her Mystery, as she stands on a crescent moon
amidst the stars, glimpsed in the background of the
Cave. The libretto is a play of the Enlightenment, por-
traying mankind's progression from chaos and superstition to Illumination. The couplet that is sung at the
completion of each of the two acts declares: "Then is
Earth a heavenly kingdom and mortality like onto the
gods". The Isis Mystery will resurface, as we shall see, in
an occultist sci-fi religion of the 20th century.

Incarnation

Just as sparks fly upward to coalesce at the outer surround of the cosmos, conversely, individual sparks from the empyrean descend for the incarnation, yearning to quench their burning thirst in the wetness of flesh. This cosmic fire is the origin of life. The sun, which lies lower than the empyrean, and the planets glowing with reflected light are gateways for the descent. They are also stages upward for the divestiture of the burden of corporeal existence as the fire returns to the empyrean. Incarnation and its opposite, ex-carnation, occur along the axis of the sacred mountain with its volcanic core, where the planetary metals are recast in the metallurgy of the soul. In Christian mythology, fire burns both in hell and in paradise.

Psychedelic experience is a journey to new realms of consciousness. The scope and content of the experience is limitless, but its characteristic features are the transcendence of verbal concepts, of space-time dimensions, and of the ego or identity. Such experiences of enlarged consciousness can occur in a variety of ways: sensory deprivation, yoga exercises, disciplined meditation, religious or aesthetic ecstasies, or spontaneously. Most recently they have become available to anyone through the ingestion of psychedelic drugs.

—Timothy Leary
Ralph Metzner
Richard Alpert
The Psychedelic Experience

The empyrean thus becomes a mythical destination, a spiritual realm conceived as a topographical place. This simplifies the matter since it makes something immaterial material. Empyrean has the verbal idea of fire in it, as in pyrotechnics, "fireworks." With the multiple metaphoric motifs symbolized by fire, the empyrean is the fiery core of consciousness, the reservoir of being, the source and home of perfected intellect, knowledge beyond division into categories. The ecstatic journey to this mythical realm affords not only knowledge or cognition, but also Platonic recognition—re-cognition—of things familiar but half forgotten. It is the ultimate secret of religions, a mystery. It is a place familiar, suggesting the notion, despite its overwhelming strangeness, that one has been there before.

Ecstasy

In Greek, ecstasy means one *stands outside* oneself, enters another dimension, a world apart. Mystics have achieved this empryrean cosmic consciousness by a variety of means: sensory deprivation, meditation, corporeal mortification, sexual abstinence, dancing, chanting, and rhythmic breathing. Sometimes the experience is spontaneous without the limits imposed upon human consciousness by the incarnation. It offers the opportunity, while still alive, to merge with the totality and to benefit from a realm not delimited by the physical dimensions of ordinary reality.

Through ecstasy, stepping out of one's wits, the Other is free to journey to distant realms, leaving the shell of the former Self behind. The ecstatic journey offers the potential for clairvoyance, shape shifting, zoomorphism, bilocation, which is the ability to inhabit two places at the same time or the projection of a double persona, the comprehension of the speech of animals or the verbal communion with the spirit of plants, and similar phenomena reported by those adept in the art. Called shamans today, these people they have had a variety of designations through-out history, including mystics, healers, witches, vision-ary philosophers, and Gnostics.

Road Map

The mythical empyrean provides a road map, a record of others who have gone there. In the 5th century BCE Parmenides described the experience as an exhilarating journey in a chariot drawn by mares to the gigantic gate through which Day and Night pass each other along a cosmic axis that reached all the way from the heavens to the netherworld, the shining column of light.

Thus another way of looking at cosmic conscious-ness is as the reunion with the totality of creation, the center of all being that birthed from the volcanic womb of Gaia or 'grew' or was 'born' as Nature—*physis* in Greek, *natura* in Latin. In this sense, the ultimate topographical goal is not the outer limits of the cosmos, but the absolute center, retrac-ing the pathway of incarnation. The underworld as a geocentric mythical topography is equally this realm of unified existence, coalescence with the primal source of all that came into being. Gaia consciousness is synonymous with the empyrean, defined differently only by another mythical topography.

Gaia conscious-ness is syn-onymous with the empyrean.

As a metaphoric destination, it requires a vehicle for the journey, like the chariot of Parmenides, an alteration in the ordinary state of mind. Myth has many ways of describing this vehicle, a vast array of miracu-lous beasts or fantastic companions to convey you to the imaginary place. Since it is only metaphorically a place, the vehicle is actually a means of altering the

What they call the tree of knowledge of good and evil, the conscious perception of the Light… it was I who brought about that they ate.

—The Words of Christ
Apocryphon of John

state of mind, but the simplest and most ancient transport is to eat the food of the gods, a sacramental plant, like the fiery herb that Prometheus stole from the jealous gods, or the fruit of the Tree in Eden, of which it was forbidden to eat.

Thus the mythical conveyances often betray attributes indicating that they are a metaphor for a botanical agent that alters consciousness, such as the winged horse Pegasus, son of the Gorgon, from whose hooves spring fountains of inspiration, or Odin's Sleipnir. In the 6th century the prophet Mohammed had such a magical horse, al-Barack, named the Bolt of Lightning and colored red with white spots. It took the enraptured prophet from the cave where he meditated in the Holy City of Mecca to the Temple Mount in Jerusalem in a single night, and thence upward to the seventh heaven.

Jesus Shining in Eden

In the 3rd century CE, a syncretistic Christian sect arose in the marshlands of the confluence of the Tigris and Euphrates rivers that survived in various forms until the 19th century. The Roman Church persecuted its adherents in medieval Europe in the Albigensian Crusade against the Cathars. It is known as Manichaeism, from the name of its prophet, and St. Augustine was originally one of its adherents. From various sources in a variety of languages, Syriac, Arabic, Persian, Chinese, Greek, Coptic, and Latin, a mythology of the magical plants of fire can be reconstructed, a mythology that probably is much more ancient and implicit in the motifs connecting the forbidden fruit with the metaphor of spiritual fire.

O happy sin that brought us such a savior.

—*Roman Missal*
Exultet Hymn

The essential doctrine is the concept of dual forces in constant battle. One is the realm of the empyreal light with its connotations of revealed knowledge or cosmic consciousness. The other is its opposite, the realm of darkness. The battle was waged as a weird dietary contest, with each side destroying the other by eating it. Whatever one side ate, however, was put at risk by sexual copulation, which was inevitably with the other side, as opposites attract. These themes of foods and sex have obvious suggestions of mystical orgasmic experience and shamanic rituals.

In order to recapture the illumination that had been engulfed by the darkness, the forces of Light created a ravishingly beautiful hermaphroditic angel called Sophia or Wisdom as the goddess Athena and sent her to seduce the agents of Darkness and bring back to the empyrean their uncontrollable ejaculations of light. In this ecstatic encounter some of their semen of stolen light missed its mark and fell by accident to earth, instead of entering the womb of Sophia and replenishing the empyrean. From this *coitus interruptus* of spilled semen sprouted the entire botanical realm of plants. All plants have empyreal light within them. They are animate with the illumination of revelation. Unlike animals and the other fleshy beings of creation, plants have escaped the entrapment of Light in the incarnation of matter. Plants don't exhibit the sin of lust.

The essential doctrine is the concept of dual forces in constant battle.

Forces of Light and Darkness

The Manichaean sect prescribed a vegetarian diet to engulf as much light as possible, and ideally refrained from sex for fear of losing it, or at least procreative sex for the highest grade of the elite. Among the plants honored, as a sacrament for this sect, the most pure, the ones with the highest concentration of illumination and fire, were the mushrooms, particularly the red ones. The psychoactive *Amanita muscaria* was reserved as a secret for only the most elite. They alone might achieve reunion with the empyrean, assisted by the sacrifices of the congregation. Unlike the other plants, which reproduce sexually, the mushrooms have no seeds and, despite their sexual metaphoric manifestations, appear to have no manner of reproduction except the fall of the bolt of light from the empyrean.

Mushrooms have no seeds and appear to have no manner of reproduction except the fall of the bolt of light from the empyrean.

In this scenario, the forces of darkness retaliated by creating Adam, the man of clay, to lock up in his incarnation their dwindling supply of stolen light. Then they nefariously created also the eternal seductress in the form of Eve. The two were set free to lust for each other as the concupiscent agents to further lock up the light with each of their ever-increasing offspring, forever diluting more and more the light in corporeal entrapment, as the race of humans proliferated.

To reverse this insidious captivity, the forces of Light sent the shining Jesus in the form of the Serpent in Eden, to urge Adam to eat of the forbidden fruit from the Tree of Knowledge. This is the fruit that replenishes the diminishing store of empyreal light.

This tradition pervades Christian mysticism throughout Europe of the medieval and Renaissance periods. Jesus is already present at the Temptation, resident in the Tree of Eden, and Eve's sin was no sin at all, but a happy fault, a blessed event or *felix culpa*, that would set the stage for the Redemption through the miraculous incarnation of the Savior in the womb of the Blessed Virgin. Jesus is the new Adam, and Mary as the Queen of Heaven is His spouse and the perfection of Eve.

Perhaps the most explicit example of this *felix culpa* is displayed in the van Eyck Ghent Altarpiece. The artist used the same model for the shockingly nude Eve and for the Virgin Annunciate and her elevation to the heavens as the Regina, married to her own resurrected Son. Similarly, the model whom he used for Adam reappears in the inner presentation of the Altarpiece as Jesus in the role of the Regina's Spouse.

In the painted ceiling of the *Michaeliskirche* in Hildesheim of Lower Saxony, Jesus is depicted resident in the Tree of Eden at the Temptation of Adam and Eve. Similarly, the Serpent, as in Hugo van der Goes's *Temptation*, is often female, as a prefiguration of the Virgin. Michelangelo depicted the serpent as a hermaphroditic coupling of Lilith and Samuel in the Sistine Chapel; and the Female Serpent became identified with the mermaid Melusina, whose antiquity can be traced back to the Gorgon Medusa.

Moses receiving the book no one could read,

Burning Bush

The Manichaean myth provides a perfect exemplar of the fire within the plant. It is such a plant on-fire that Moses encountered as a burning bush, a fire that did not consume the bush and from which issued the voice of the Lord. Mount Sinai, which is also called Horeb, may not be the mountain now identified in the Sinai. Its biblical description is more appropriate for a volcano, and some scholars locate it in the Arabian Peninsula. In the biblical account, the summit was clouded with smoke.

There are two versions of *Genesis*, neither obviously written by Moses, at least not in Hebrew, since the Phoenician letters were not invented until five hundred years later. The entire Pentateuch could only have survived as oral teaching, and actually biblical scholarship today ascribes a variety of dates to its constituent parts. Whatever it was that Moses took down from Mount Sinai, the two stone tablets were not written in Hebrew, and if they were, there would have been no one who knew how to read them. Of course, as a prince of Egypt, Moses would have learned hieroglyphics. Since he didn't take the blank tablets up to the mountain, it is likely that they were something he found up there, with markings that looked like Egyptian.

The *Exodus* account makes clear that the tablets preserved in the Ark of the Covenant, and which few ever saw, are reproductions or replacements for the original tablets that Moses destroyed. In later historical revisionism by the priesthood, Moses also is supposed to have received a lengthy legal document, detailing the terms for the relationship of Yahweh with his chosen people.

The motif of the book of knowledge imparted by God is a commonplace, as we shall see, in the shamanic experience of transcendence, and quite often the person who receives is not capable of reading it. All that is required is to eat it.

Often the person who receives the book of knowledge is not capable of reading it. All that is required is to eat it.

The second section of *Genesis*, which contains the episode of the forbidden fruit, was composed in the 8th century BCE as part of the patriarchal denigration of the female. Eve was earlier a version of the widespread Canaanite, Anatolian, and Mesopotamian goddess. The first *Genesis*, with its theme of the Light and without the prohibition, was later, probably in the 4th century BCE and influenced by neo-Platonism.

The Book No One Can Read

This fruit, like a burning bush, that can access the empyrean or the womb of the Cosmic Mother, a plant that alters consciousness to its boundless universal dimension can be called a drug only by someone who intends to devalue the experience as hallucinatory, not real, a fiction of a medically incapacitated mind. Because of the prejudice against drugs and their recreational and addictive misuse, a new word was required to recognize the great potential they offer for spiritual development and access to paranormal cognitive and physical abilities

Entheogen designates a sacramental plant that was considered to be animate, a food consubstan-

tial with the 'spirit' of deity, on-fire with a spark
from the empyrean. Combining the ancient Greek
adjective *entheos*—inspired, animate with deity—
and the verbal root in *genesis*—becoming, it signi-
fies "something that causes the divine to reside
within one."

3

⊘RIGINS OF ℛELIGION

ave drawings and the related phallic stone pillars indicate that entheogens were at the origins of humankind's spiritual awakening. Plato's Myth of the Cave is the most enduring paradigm for the journey to the empyrean. An earlier version of it from the mythical inheritance of oral tradition is the Cave of the Cyclops in the Homeric Odyssey. Entheogens can be shown as the origins, not only of the oldest religions, but also of new ones now being formed. Psychoactive sacraments are not a sign of decadence, but of the earliest occurrences, later strenuously denied by the official theology and reserved for its ecclesiastical elite.

On the Wall of the Cave

Humans have left a record of cognitive experiences dating back to the first emergence of *Homo sapiens* in the late Paleolithic Age roughly 32,000 years ago. This period is characterized by the creation of tools and weapons, but also by paintings in caves and rock shelters, which indicate a spiritual awareness at the very dawn of the distinct hominid species. Since the paintings require some preconceptions for their interpretation, investigators often prefer merely to record their occurrence rather than to burden them with religious significance or compare them with rituals still practiced today after the passage of so many millennia. Religion is unscientific. This is unfortunate, since it defines humans at their origin as materialistic manipulators of their environment, without communion with its indwelling spirits. The species is named *Homo sapiens*, whereas perhaps spiritualis would be better.

The paintings have common themes. They also often occur in situations that made their creation extremely difficult, in dark subterranean chambers nearly inaccessible, suggesting that they may have been the sites for sacred ceremonies for which the paintings were either the result, as a record of experience, or more probably created at considerable effort as an aid for accessing such experience. The caves were not used as ordinary dwellings and are totally unsuited for habitation. The animals depicted are often large honorific wild beasts, not necessarily, however, the most typical prey of the actual hunt, as indicated by bone deposits of beasts eaten or sacrificed in the surrounding areas.

Aquatic animals like fish and turtles are also depicted from areas as distant as Siberia and Africa. Other themes are male or female hunters and dancers, indicating the ecstatic nature of the hunt or more probably the preparation or interpretation of the actual hunt. One famous scene from Lascaux depicts what is apparently a shaman, with a bird-topped scepter, who has fallen prostrate into a trance that he has accessed apparently by something metaphorically depicted as a bull anally transfixed by a spear. This is not a likely hunting scene.

Hybrid Creatures

The paintings were probably not intended as magic to encourage the abundance of the herds roaming outside, but as a means of empowerment, accessing communion

and spiritual empathy with the beasts, including the
aquatic ones. Zoomorphism, combining the animal's features with the human, yields mythical creatures like bull-
men—the Cretan Minotaur), antlered men—the Celtic
Cernunnos, goat men—satyrs, horsemen—centaurs, and
aquatic mermen and mermaids—Gorgons, tritons.

In later art, this motif is represented by the configuration of the Anatolian mistress of beasts or potnia theron,
of great Minoan antiquity. Although as Artemis she is a
hunter, she is the animals' patron and exacts vengeance
upon anyone who slaughters her protected animal or
inadvertently stumbles upon her and her entitled entou-
rage in the hunt. In the case of the goddess Artemis or
Diana, this happens while they are bathing, suggesting
that they derive from half-aquatic manifestations. In the
myth of the sacri-
fice of Iphigenia,
the maiden is a by-
name of the god-
dess as a birthing
midwife, and she
substitutes a doe
at the last minute
upon the altar.

Satyr–goat-man
and faun–deer-
man, dancing,
with drinking cup
and a panther, the
animal familiar
of the god of
ecstasy.

The same
theme occurs
with the hunter Actaeon, who intrudes upon the hunt
of the goddess. Artemis turns him into a stag, the prey
of the hunt, dismembered by his own pack of hounds.
Although a perpetual virgin, Artemis is interchangeable with menstruating females, the wet-nurse, and the
midwife.

Subterranean Ecstasy

Painted handprints and finger flutings have recently
been identified as female, rather than male, some quite
young as indicated by the small size and low elevation
from the ground; and figurines of the Venus type suggest
that birthing women played an essential role, perhaps as
initiators for pubescent males or females. The so-called
Venus of Willendorf is remarkable for the thinness of
her arms, despite the corpulence of her maternal body.
She also has no face, merely a cap, with a scabby coif-
fure arranged in seven concentric circles. She is probably best described as an anthropomorphized Amanita
fairy, with her skinny arms masquerading as the annulus
ring, the remnants of the shattered spore membrane.

Among indigenous people today who still enact
cave rites, women and men have separate caves. The
cave is seen as the site of their tribe's primordial emergence from the ground, the home of their ancestors,
and the place where their most secret myth is retold.
The handprints are interpreted as proof of their ancient ancestry, and new ones are traced in the course
of bloody puberty rituals. If there is a common theme
in all these paintings worldwide, it is probably religious
ceremonies of a shamanic or initiatory type.

Human zoomorphism in these paintings almost
certainly indicates shamanic rituals. Certain paintings,
in particular those from the Tassili n'Ajjer Saharan
plateau in Algeria, also suggest the involvement of
entheogens in the ceremonies. One shows an antlered
male with a bee mask and a body sprouting multiple
mushrooms. Mush-
rooms replace his
fingers and there is

Human zoomorphism in these
paintings almost certainly
indicates shamanic rituals

a handprint tracing next to his antlers. Others depict women warriors with 'round heads,' fungal caps spotted with white, suggesting the identity of the mushrooms as *Amanita muscaria.*

Paintings from Indonesia develop the motif of the bee-hunter as a psychoactive experience. Recently, Earl Lee has connected the motif of honey in these paintings with the cult of the dead and the incorporation of the corpse as a medium for the growth or fermentation of toxic additives to psychoactive potions. The ritual appears to have been Egyptian and imported into Minoan Crete. It is reflected in Latin traditions of swarms of bees emerging from the putrefying hide of a slaughtered bull. In addition to other possible fermented toxins, the corpse, as in the Tassili depiction of the bee shaman, provides a medium for the growth of mushrooms.

Mushroom Children

The fungal anthropomorphisms might be compared to the petroglyphs from the cliff faces above the Pegtymel River in the Chukota region of far-eastern Siberia. They date probably to the 1st millennium BCE and portray tiny

Everything was going well. His wife gave birth to a son. Then Czelkutq left for the woods, where he met some pretty little mushroom-girls. He stayed with them and forgot his wife.

—Siberian folktale

females with mushroom crowns, engaging in a ritual dance, in a context with reindeer, wolves, a kayak, fish, and seals. The little girls are leading the hunt, but as children, that is an unlikely reality. They are anthropomorphisms of mushrooms.

María Sabina: I see the mushrooms as children, as clowns, children with violins, children with trumpets, child-clowns who sing and dance around me, children tender as sprouts, as flower buds.

—R. Gordon Wasson,
Wondrous Mushroom

Siberian folk-tales record that these little girls are found on the forest floor and are apt to seduce people into a trance that makes them forget their way back home. Another myth identifies them as wapaq spirits, with red hats, spotted with the spittle of the god who caused them to grow from the ground. In Nordic myth, the spittle of Odin's horses similarly engenders the mushrooms. They endowed the culture hero Big Raven with superior strength. This is an attribute accorded to the *Amanita muscaria*, as in the battle rituals of the Nordic Berserkers. These latter materialized on the battlefield as wolves, although they are named as wearing the skin of a bear. The Koryak Big Raven—Quyqinyaqu—is a trickster like Prometheus, and he appears across the Bering Straits as Coyote and other figures in the indigenous folklore of the North American Indians.

The Siberian tale bears comparison to the myth of the sun mushroom of the indigenous Northeastern American Algonquin nation. There, Younger Brother journeys to the subterranean otherworld and returns as an ecstatic anthropomorphism of the *Amanita muscaria*, with a cure for every ailment in the form of his psychoactive urine. Petroglyphs from the American Southwest document similar anthropomorphisms with a variety of psychoactive plants. The urine as a psychoactive metabolite is a theme worldwide where the active agent is the *Amanita muscaria*.

Urine is commonly linked to reindeer and other stags because

Every time the clouds darken the moon, he urinates. The People drink this liquid that has been given to them as a great boon by the Sun Mushroom spirits.

of the inordinate fondness of the Cervidae species for grazing on the mushroom, which leads them to attack anyone urinating the metabolite. The flesh of the deer that has ingested the mushroom is similarly psycho-active, and hence the deer hunt is analogous to the picking of the fungal agent. It would be impossible not to see a reflection of this special role of the Cervidae in the myths about Artemis, especially since she is associated with the Ceryneian hind, a female deer with a golden antler. The only antlered does are reindeer.

Bull Dancers

In southern Spain in the Selva Pasquala near Cuenca, quite a few of the rock shelters have paintings, some dating back to around 6,000 BCE. They may actually be earlier than the Tassili n'Ajjer paintings, and this whole region of northern Africa and southern Spain once shared a much more luxurious forestation in Paleolithic times. A rock shelter is a cliff

The flesh of the deer that has ingested the mush-room is similarly psychoac-tive, and hence the deer hunt is analogous to the picking of the fungal agent.

wall protected by a rocky overhang. One particularly fine example is part of a total complex with related paintings on the other side of a natural fissure through the mountaintop. The totality indicates that the place was used as a sacred site related to solstice ceremonies, perhaps as a solar calculator.

Myths are traditional tales of extraordinary antiquity, existing long before they surface in written form, and traceable in many cases back to rituals of primordial shamanism.

In one spot, the rock surface has a natural configuration that, like a hallucination emerging from the stone, suggests the form of a bull. Like something materialized from a vision, the artist has summoned this into a remarkably fine painting of the animal. At the base line to the right, thirteen creatures, apparently dancing and hence ecstatic, are anthropomorphized mushrooms, probably of the psychoactive *Psilocybe* species, the *hispanica* with its characteristic crooked stipe. The number thirteen is significant as the approximate number of lunar cycles in a solar year.

Other depictions in the scene include an ithyphallic archer, more indicative of the ecstatic nature of the experience than of the actual hunt. He is shooting at a configuration above the bull that may be a depiction of the constellation Orion, suggesting a cosmological referent. In Greek mythology, Orion was born from a bull's carcass on which the gods had urinated. His father was a beekeeper. Myths are traditional tales of extraordinary antiquity, existing long before they surface in written form, and traceable in many cases back to rituals of primordial shamanism. Hence the nativity of Orion may well be a version of the cult of the dead and the engendering of the honey drink from the ferments of corpses. This is a fungal growth traditionally associated with the bull.

Another scene depicts a horse being led around in a circle. This may or may not be related to the bull episode, or added at some other time. Other depictions in the bull episode are too weathered to decipher. Additional doodles and graffiti suggest that the site was reused over a long period of time, some indicating its continuance in some way into the Christian era, not necessarily, however, as anything more than a place of rendezvous in the forest.

Womb and Phallus

The pillars are natural phallic structures and complement the womb-like enclosure of the caves.

The prehistoric cave paintings are probably related to the very numerous rock pillars, termed dolmens and menhirs, found throughout Europe and Eurasia. Their remarkable resemblance to mushrooms sometimes shows evidence that the similarity was further enhanced through human intervention. Sometimes the dolmens are anthropomorphized phalluses. The addition of Christian crosses indicates the assimilation of pagan traditions into the new religion.

Similar designs serve as the architectural model for tombs, particularly in Etruscan necropolises and in India, and more simply as common grave markers in Greece and Anatolia. The pillars are obviously natural phallic structures and are the complement of the womb-like enclosure of the caves. They symbolize the two aspects of the Earth's sexuality.

Subterranean altar chamber with dolmens, Isle of Guernsey

Permeable Walls

Paintings in caves and rock shelters, like the decoration of Egyptian tombs, are an evocation of the outside world and are meant both to summon a remembrance of it into the enclosure and to function as a permeable pathway for the journey of the spirit through the barrier to the world beyond. In the recently discovered Chauvet cave in southern France, paintings dating from the Paleolithic seem to elicit animals from the rock configuration, including a bull approaching a rock formation made into the likeness of a female's genitalia.

The motif of the cave as the crucible for transcendence seems to trace far back into prehistory.

Caves are a magical locale for metaphysical birthing and for the shamanic transport to the realm we have summarized as the mythical topography of the column linking Gaia with the empyrean. Thus the motif of the cave as the crucible for transcendence seems to trace far back into prehistory.

In later religious rites, like Zoroastrian Mithraism, the entheogen-induced initiation progressed from a re-imagining of the initial incarnation from the fiery cosmos via the cooling lunar intermediary for the descent into the cave sanctuary. The seven sequential grades of initiation reversed the incarnation, culminating in the eventual final bursting from the subterranean chamber for the reunion with the solar deity in the realm of the empyrean. The roof of the subterranean sanctuary was sometimes painted with a map of the starry firmament. This suggests the amazing longevity of a primordial human programming, perhaps inevitable on a planet dependent upon the light and heat of the sun.

Medieval and Renaissance churches were intended similarly as gateways to the world beyond, channeling astrological phenomena by an evocation of potent symbolic forms into a talismanic configuration, simultaneously aligning the enclosed space with the cosmos or the empyrean and coaxing the planetary bodies into a propitious rearrangement. The ancient Greek temple had a similar relationship to the cosmos and the entheogen that afforded access to it. A temple is named as a designated space on earth for observing the heavens, and the design of a Greek temple, with its surround of columnar trees or pillars, is an architectural imitation of a sacred forest, on whose floor might be found the sacred plant stylized in the Ionic capital as a cross section of the curving cap atop the trunk-like stipe of a mushroom.

It would be easier to accept these as *phalloi* if any one of them bore the slightest resemblance to the organ with which Greek artists were well familiar. The asymmetry of the *glans*, and the duct and testicles are never shown, and the knob is often flat, hemispherical or spherical. The only group of objects which all these *phalloi* can be said to resemble is fungi.

—Kurt and Boardman
Greek Burial Customs.

The First Supper

Peter Webster argued that before the Last Supper, commemorated by the Christian Eucharist, there was a First Supper, mythologized by the Tree in Eden. Either driven by hunger to experiment with novel foods, or perhaps expressly directed by a shaman capable

Peter Webster asserts there was a First Supper, mythologized by the Tree in Eden.

A prodigious expansion in Man's memory must have been the gift that differentiated mankind from his predecessors, and I surmise that this expansion in memory led to a simultaneous growth in the gift of language, these two powers generating in man that self-consciousness which is the third of the triune traits that alone make man unique. Those three gifts—memory, language and self-consciousness—so interlock that they seem inseparable, the aspects of a quality that permitted us to achieve all the wonders we now know.

—R. Gordon Wasson
Persephone's Quest

of communing with the indwelling spirit of the entheogen, humankind experienced a heightened level of consciousness that spurred the rapid dominance of the species over its competitors among the earth's creatures. The evidence suggests that the evolution was not gradual, but triggered by some event that dramatically changed the species and led to the spread of culture out of Africa. This could well have been a spiritual awareness induced by eating the fruit of the First Supper. The archaeological record shows a sudden increase in the size of the cranial capacity. Such a change is generally assumed to indicate increased cognitive ability.

Terrence McKenna proposed a similar theory, suggesting that the entheogen provided some physical advantage, like improved visual acuity or bodily strength, both of which are possible effects from certain drugs. These improvements, however, as acquired characteristics, would not be inheritable, whereas a spiritual awakening leading to religious indoctrination would become perpetuated in the formation of a cultural identity. It is such a shamanic event that seems to lie at the origin of the later tales of gods and heroes and their interaction in the affairs of humankind.

The Myth of the Cave

Plato mythologized this visionary event with the parable of the cave. The eye is unique as an organ of perception in that it sees only through the instrumentality of illumination. Imagine that people are chained in a cave, forced to view only the fleeting shadows projected upon the blank wall, cast by objects that move behind them illumined by a fire. The shaman teacher, which the Greeks termed a philosopher, drags these prisoners, content with what they see, unwillingly up the steep incline to the mouth of the cave and the daylight of the outside world. At first they are blinded by the painful brilliance, rejecting what they see as less real than the familiar shadows on the wall of the cave. The message, applied to those of us who live in what we consider the light, is that beyond this shadow world of appearances is another realm where true reality exists. This realm is the empyrean.

The Greeks termed the shaman teacher a philosopher.

Another Greek version of the cave myth is the Homeric account of Odysseus in the Cave of the Cyclops, a primordial man with a single eye. Odysseus drugs the giant with a powerful intoxicant and then puts out the sight of the cave dweller's eye with a burning timber. He cleverly has told the monster that his name is Nobody. The Cyclops, in contrast, bears the name of Famous, Polyphemus. Nobody and Somebody are obviously related as an antithetical dichotomy. When the blinded Cyclops calls for help, he shouts that Nobody is hurting him, and therefore his fellow tribesmen pay no regard. Upon escaping from the cave, Odysseus calls out his true name, which earns him the 'hatred' of his victim and the unfailing enmity of his father, Poseidon, the god of the seas. It is this enmity that makes Odysseus Somebody, the famous hero of the *Odyssey*.

The naming motif is characteristic of an initiatory rite, where one loses the former persona by becoming no one, before emerging from the nadir of existence with the new identity, Odysseus as the hero of the Trojan War. The truer etymology of the hero's name, however, is not the 'hated foe,' but an epithet of the bear, 'floppy-ear,' whose hibernation in a cave sets the pattern for apparent death and resurrection. 'Nobody' in the Greek in this context has two forms, both metis and outis. The former also means 'intelligence,' and the latter in its Homeric dialectal form of otis is 'floppy-ear.' Indeed, an Etruscan version of the Odysseus story claimed that the reason for the hero's long disappearance from this conscious world was simply that he got so tired that he fell asleep. A similar theme is basic to the whole tradition of the epic homecomings, which are called a nostos as the return to the nous or perceiving, awakened mind. In the *Odyssey*, Odysseus finally falls asleep on a magical boat and wakes up back home.

Primordial man might well have modeled the religious rites of the cave on the pattern observed in the sleeping bear, with which they sometimes shared the shelter. To prepare for hibernation, the bear eats voraciously, including psychoactive mushrooms. In Greek mythology, the bear is metaphorically a bee-eater, associated with the honey-drink, the ferment of bull carcasses, and an attribute of Artemis, whose other animal familiar, as we have seen, is the deer. The bear, world-wide, has a special significance, since it walks upright like a human. It is fantasized that within its hulking frame lies a human, captured or pos-sessed, so that the killing of the bear is a sacred liberation. The bear, moreover, seems to reinforce its easy confusion with the human since the male beast is aroused by a woman's pheromone.

Odysseus escaping from
the Cave of the Cyclops

In the Homeric account of Odysseus's emergence from the cave of the Cyclops, the hero actually must disguise himself as an animal to escape. He ties himself beneath a ram in the monster's herd. The rock blocking the entrance to the cave is too heavy for the hero to dislodge by himself, but the monstrous Cyclops moves it aside to allow his animals out to graze, running his fingers over the rams' fleece to check that none of the captive men is escaping, but unaware that the bottom half of the fleece is the hero and his surviving companions

Several caves in Thrace are identified by folk tradition as the original cave of Polyphemus. They appear from the distance to resemble a face, but on closer observation, the dual openings that at first are taken as the eyes actually suggest that the intervening nose is really a stipe, while the hemispherical forehead above makes a good likeness of the mushroom's cap.

The fleece of the ram in the trick that Odysseus plays on his opponent is a frequent metaphor for the scabby cap of the *Amanita muscaria*. The best-known

example is the golden fleece of the ram that the hero
Jason plucks from a magical tree. This means that in
this episode Odysseus has essentially become a mushroom to escape from his initiatory cave. The tribe of
Cyclopes, moreover, as we have seen, is the workmen in the volcanic crucible of Hephaestus, forging the thunderbolts of Zeus. Their one-eyed attribute suggests the disembodied eye of transcendent vision. Tradi-

> The fleece of the ram in the trick that Odysseus plays on his opponent is a fre-quent metaphor for the scabby cap of the Amanita muscaria.

tionally, there are three of them, each named with an
epithet of the thunderbolt.

Both the cave of the philosopher Plato, with its
great antiquity traceable back to the permeable painted
walls of the Paleolithic womb of the cave and the pillar
symbolism, and that of Odysseus's Cyclops are based
on the ecstatic entheogen-induced transcendence that
lies at the origins of religion. As part of the epic oral
tradition, the story of Odysseus encodes ritual themes
from the earliest times. Plato's version derives from this
archaic ritual, reinforced by the use of caves in his own
time for shamanic incubation and transcendent vision.

An Archaic Technique of Ecstasy

Shamanism became a more familiar type of religious
experience through the revolution of the psychedelic
60s. The word originally designated only a type of priest
among certain Siberian Mongolian peoples and was
restricted to the anthropological study of their culture.
People we now identify as shamans were previously
pejoratively called witchdoctors, or in their own indigenous cultures known as wise men or women and

healers. The Romanian scholar Mircea Eliade wrote
what was the exhaustive, definitive study of shamanism
as *Archaic Techniques of Ecstasy*. He amply documented
the role played by drugs in accessing this archaic ecstasy. He, moreover, had personally experimented with
a variety of drugs, including mescaline, passionflower,
opium, and methamphetamine, as stimulants for both
mystical and creative inspiration.

Nevertheless, he surprisingly came to condemn
drugs as indicative only of the late decadent stages of
religion. He authoritatively pronounced that entheogens were not at the origin of religion, even though
this would be the simplest and most natural way for
primordial man to achieve the ecstatic experience. In
doing this, he was responding with distaste to the irresponsible recreational drug use he encountered among
his students. Eliade thus retarded the study of shamanism and added his voice to the growing concern about
contemporary drug abuse. In his view, a shaman like
the Mazatec María Sabina was not a perpetuation of an
archaic technique, surviving in a culture marginalized
by the main stream of history, but its recent extension
to what he called 'lower peoples or social groups'. The
term is obviously prejudicial. When confronted with his
condemnation in an interview shortly before his death,
he appeared disturbed, too old to begin something new.

In contrast, entheogens, as the cave paintings indicate, were at the very origin of the religious awareness
of *Homo spiritualis*. The denigration of the entheogen
seems, in contrast, to be characteristic of the decadent
stages, when the sacrament is deemed too dangerous
for the lower class of peoples or social groups, and is
reserved only for the elite with proper preparation.
The deity becomes the property of the priesthood, and

Only certain of the highest hierarchy are admitted to the secret of the most archaic technique, which lay at the very origins of religion.

the congregation is taught that a placebo will afford the transcendent communion for anyone hardy enough to undertake the rigors of a spiritual life. The church lays claim to the empyrean and colonizes it as the province of its clergy. Only certain of the highest hierarchy are admitted to the secret of the most archaic technique, which lay at the very origins of religion.

In fact, Eliade confided to Peter Furst that he had come to accept that there was no essential difference between ecstasy achieved by plant hallucinogens and that obtained by other archaic techniques.

4

TOXIC EUCHARIST

It would appear, in fact, that an entheogen was at the origin, not only of primordial religion, but also of the most basic rite of Christianity. A strange event in Corinth at the very inception of Christianity has gone unnoticed, although it is recorded in one of the assuredly authentic documents about the earliest days of the Church. About the year 59, Paul reprimands the congregation he had founded in Corinth about a decade earlier for not performing the Eucharist correctly. Because of this, quite a few people have taken sick, and quite a few have even died. It is highly unlikely that they died from eating too much holy bread and communion wine.

Paul's is the earliest account of the Eucharist as a sacred ceremony. The gospel accounts do not specify that the Last Supper should form the nucleus of the religious gatherings, and in any case, they were written down after Paul and would have been revised or backdated. In the 2nd century history of the Church, known as the Acts of the Apostles, we learn only that the apostles met daily to take their meals. This is ordinary food, not a sacrament.

Intoxication by drugs seems not to have formed part of the original practice. The use of narcotics is indicative of the decadence of a technique of ecstasy or of its extension to lower peoples or social groups.

—Mircea Eliade
Shamanism

The next-earliest authentic document about the early Church is Pliny's investigation of the troublesome Christian community in his Anatolian province for the Emperor Hadrian. He reports that the Christians eat their meals together, just ordinary food, innocuous food. This could mean that they are not cannibals in eating their God, or babies, or that there was some suspicion abroad that they ate something special and toxic. He reports, however, that the meal came later in the day, and that they met at dawn to salute the rising sun. This was the essence of their rite. If they ate the Eucharist, it would have been part of this ceremony, rather than their daily bread. It is unlikely also that the special Eucharist was a daily event, since it would incapacitate them for the ensuing workday.

Paul, moreover, explains the Eucharist as a mystery, which for his Greek audience would inevitably be understood in terms of the great initiation celebrated just a few miles up the coast in the village of Eleusis, where a psychoactive potion was the essence of the experience. The cavernous Telesterion or hall of initiation was carved out of the bedrock side of the acropolis

Sanctuary of Aphrodite on the Sacred Road to Eleusis

of the village. It is not a traditional Greek temple, but an architectural reconstruction of a subterranean cave, from which a great illumination was said to burst at the moment of the

ritual's culmination. If Paul did actually invent the
Eucharist as a Christian ceremony, which is likely, he
may have modeled it upon his probable induction into
Mithraism, since he came from Tarsus, a stronghold of
the new religion, and his wealthy family was assimilated
into Hellenic culture and had dealings with the Roman
army. Mithraism had some kind of holy bread that was a
metaphor for a psychoactive agent.

As someone educated in Hellenism, moreover, he
would also have been knowledgeable about neo-Platonism, which he in fact references in this same letter
in his famous metaphor of the true reality that is seen
only as a reflection in a faulty mirror, through a glass
darkly. This is blatantly a reference to Plato's myth of
the Cave. As a philhellene, Paul may well have even
been initiated at Eleusis.

As a Jew, moreover, he would have been well aware
of the traditions of the magical Mosaic food of manna.
Christ is the new manna that comes down from heaven.
Paul would also know full well that the holy chrism of
Judaism, which Christ as the 'Anointed' inherits, was
a powerful combination of psychoactive substances.
The precise formula is specified in Exodus and the main
ingredient is cannabis. It was also burned as incense to
fumigate the enclosed space of the inner tabernacle of
the Temple in Jerusalem. The chrism was the ordina-
tion anointment of the priesthood and the fumigated
Tabernacle was something that only the High Priest
experienced and on one day alone, on Yom Kippur.

The toxic Eucharist must have been an entheogen, and Paul condemns its abuse. Whoever eats the
'bread' and drinks the 'wine' without recognizing the
in-dwelling Deity is damned. The Corinthian congregation apparently has been using the Body and Blood as a
recreational drug.

Mystical Experience

A drug is not necessary for a mystical experience. Albert Hoffman caught a glimpse of the empyrean in a spontaneously generated rift in the cosmic fabric while a teenager walking in the Alps. St. Teresa of Calcutta had a single experience while riding on a train, and spent the rest of her life devastated by a feeling of abandonment, since she never felt it again. An entheogen is not required. It provides a reliable access, however,

> Whoever eats and drinks the Eucharist without recognizing the Body is condemned.
>
> —Paul
> First Letter to the Corinthians

as would be needed for initiatory ceremonies where a group of people are expected to have a visionary experience together at the same time. At Eleusis, several thousand initiates had the transcendent experience together on schedule annually after drinking a special potion.

When Hofmann accidentally discovered LSD years later in 1943, he felt that the substance was calling out to him from the shelf in the laboratory where it had been discarded as something without further interest after the testing five years earlier. After his initial fear that he might have fatally poisoned himself, he came to realize that it was the same experience as the moment on the mountain, but with practice it deepened and could be controlled. With the German novelist Ernst Jünger, he sought out marvelous journeys of the soul to exotic lands.

Although the Eleusinian initiation could be repeated, it was a rare occurrence to be initiated more than once. The considerable expense would have been a detriment for some people, but the ancient testimony indicates that once was enough to last a lifetime. Once seen, the mystical vision suffices as a lifelong enrichment, something to be anticipated as enriching the final moments of breath. One could live one's life without fear, knowing how it would end.

The Good Friday Experiment

In 1962, Walter Pahnke, a graduate student at Harvard Divinity School, conducted a double-blind experiment, supervised by Timothy Leary, with a group of divinity students from the Boston area. The experiment was conducted in Marsh Chapel at Boston University. The event has come to be known as the Marsh Chapel Experiment or the Good Friday Experiment. A double-blind experiment means that

It happened on a May morning—I have forgotten the year—but I can still point to the exact spot where it occurred, on a forest path on Martinsberg above Baden, Switzerland. As I strolled through the freshly greened woods filled with bird song and lit up by the morning sun, all at once everything appeared in an uncommonly clear light. Was this something I had simply failed to notice before? Was I suddenly discovering the spring forest as it actually looked? It shone with the most beautiful radiance, speaking to the heart, as though it wanted to encompass me in its majesty. I was filled with an indescribable sensation of joy, oneness, and blissful security. I have no idea how long I stood there spellbound. But I recall the anxious concern I felt as the radiance slowly dissolved and I hiked on.

—Albert Hoffman
LSD: My Problem Child

half the group is administered some agent and the other half a placebo, and neither the subjects nor the testers know which group received what. This is a standard procedure in order to eliminate prejudicial suggestion for both the subjects and the administrators.

It was assumed that students of divinity would have some inkling of what constituted a religious experience since they had chosen to devote their lives to religion. Half the group received psilocybin, the psychoactive chemical in *Psilocybe* mushrooms, the other half niacin— Vitamin B, which at high dosage produces physiological changes similar to the onset of a psychedelic experience, but does not result in the visionary state. The subjects who received psilocybin reported experiencing what they interpreted as a profound religious event.

Walter Pahnke went on to become a minister, physician, and psychiatrist, working with entheogens as therapy for alcoholism, neurosis, and terminal life anxiety, until his accidental death in a diving incident in 1971. He was a member of the original team at the Maryland Psychiatric Research Center, which included Stanislav Grof, Bill Richards, and Richard Yensin. Huston Smith, the respected scholar of world religions, participated in the experiment.

Similar on-going experiments, beginning in 2006, have been conducted at Johns Hopkins University by

> I have a stronger desire for devotion; have increased yoga practice and prayer. I need less food to make me full. My alcohol use has diminished dramatically. I think I'm even warmer towards people and more accepting. I now believe I have something important to tell people about how the universe works.
>
> —Volunteer comment
> Johns Hopkins experiment

a team with foundational support and directed by Roland R. Griffiths, with similar results. The volunteers were given preliminary guidance and four different dosages of psilocybin and one of a placebo in five successive sessions, each a month apart. Most participants reported that the positive effects increased with increased dosages and that the experience ranked among the topmost spiritually significant events of their life.

> Man has closed himself up, till he sees all things thro' narrow chinks of his cavern. If the doors of perception were cleansed every thing would appear to man as it is, infinite.
>
> —William Blake
> *Marriage of Heaven and Hell*

Continuing research is documenting the therapeutic benefit of such drugs as LSD, DMT, MDMA, ibogaine, and ketamine, among others, but such work is severely restricted by the difficulty of licensing approval from the concerned governmental agencies.

Doors of Perception

British-born American novelist Aldous Huxley presented the now classic description of the psychedelic experience in his 1954 *The Doors of Perception*, which takes its title from William Blake's poem *The Marriage of Heaven and Hell*. In it, Huxley details his mescaline trip, which took place over the course of an afternoon, with visions both purely aesthetic and deeply sacramental, which he likens to the experience of Christian mystics. Mescaline is the principal agent in the peyote cactus, which was first isolated by the German pharmacologist Arthur Heffner in 1891. He was the first of a succession of scientists, psychiatrists, and anthropologists to investigate its hallucinatory effects. William

To most people who are even moderately experienced with entheogens, concepts such as awe, sacredness, eternity, grace, *agapé,* transcendence, transfiguration, dark night of the soul, born-again, heaven, and hell are more than theological ideas; they are experiences.

—Thomas B. Roberts
Professor Emeritus

Blake's poem references the Platonic Cave, man seeing "all things through the narrow chinks of his cavern."

The British psychiatrist Humphry Osmond admizistered Huxley's dosage. It was he who invented the term psychedelic, which he proposed at a meeting of the New York Academy of Sciences in 1957. Huxley had sent Osmond a rhyme with his own suggested term: "To make this trivial world sublime, take half a gram of phanerothyme." Osmond responded: "To fathom Hell or soar angelic, just take a pinch of psychedelic."

The ditty encompasses the two directions for the soul's journey and the dangers of the trip without a road map. The complete title of Huxley's book is *The Doors of Perception and Heaven and Hell,* the latter being the second essay.

What characterized Huxley's vision was that objects took on meaning, acquired salience. He saw the Platonic forms outside the cave, what the German mystic Meister Eckhart termed Istigkeit, 'Is-ness,' Being What Is: "A bunch of flowers shining with their own inner light and all but quivering under the pressure of the significance with which they were charged." "Things were nothing more and nothing less than what they were, a transience that was eternal life, a perpetual perishing that was at the same time pure Being, a bundle of minute, unique particulars in which, by some unspeakable and yet self-evident paradox, was to be seen, the divine source of all existence."

Into a Vacuum

The Psychedelic Revolution engendered a need for modes of interpreting the mystical experience. The fierce condemnation of John Allegro's work made Judeo-Christianity a hostile area and forced investigators to the margins of serious scholarship. Officially, there were no drugs in Christianity. The rich traditions of Classical mythology that could have offered a paradigm of the shamanic initiatory journey were similarly declared off-limits for anyone intending to have a successful professional career. The role of a psychoactive potion at the Eleusinian Mystery is neither discussed nor rejected in the standard treatments of Greek mythology. It simply does not exist.

Wasson was expressly warned against seeking mushrooms among the ancient Greeks. Robert Graves, the English poet and novelist, was Wasson's friend and advisor on Classical scholarship. He had known Wasson ever since he had contacted him about the mushroom poisoning of the Emperor Claudius for his novel *I, Claudius*. Graves published the Louvre bas-relief from Pharsalos in northwest Greece depicting Demeter and Persephone holding a mushroom as the cover of his *Greek Myths*, and he identified the sacrament of the Eleusin-

I do not think that Mycenae had anything to do with the divine mushroom or the Eleusinian mysteries either. May I add a word of warning? Stick to your Mexican mushroom cult and beware of seeing mushrooms everywhere. We much enjoyed your Philadelphia paper and would recommend that you keep as close to that as you can. Forgive the frankness of an old friend.

—Letter
R. Gordon Wasson archives

ian Mystery as a mushroom in his *Food for Centaurs*, but he was deemed too "individual and unconventional" to deserve professional consideration. Graves retaliated by commenting that Classical scholars lacked "the poetic capacity to forensically examine mythology."

There is a neo-pagan attempt to revive the ancient gods in Greece, known as the religion of the twelve gods, but it faces fierce rejection by the Christian Orthodox Church; and its adherents must shield their identities to avoid discrimination in the labor market. The ancient sanctuaries, moreover, are protected as archaeological sites. Any rebuilding of even the most minor shine is forbidden as altering the historical record.

To fill the vacuum created in the Judeo-Christian Hellenic-Roman tradition, many people sought paradigms in more exotic mythologies from cultures further afield. Historians of religion describe the years of the Psychedelic Revolution as a marketplace for religions. Buddhism and Hinduism seemed attractive alternatives, since the Soma sacrament is still today recognized as something intended to be psychoactive and Buddhist monks admitted that LSD induced an experience like nirvana, something not claimed as the sole property of a deity. Buddha is not a god, but merely someone who has attained enlightenment, and there are many Buddhas.

As further evidence that the original Soma was a mushroom, Wasson examined the supposed "Last Meal of the Buddha". According to what is probably an authentic historical account, around the year 483 BCE, Siddhartha Gautama, the supreme enlightened one known as the first Buddha, accepted a dish of mushrooms prepared for him by a blacksmith, and fell violently ill. There is no suspicion that the mushrooms were poisonous. The unlikely role of a blacksmith as the culinary chef suggests an alchemical theme and perhaps indicates an element of mythologized history with a volcanic crucible.

Siddhartha was on his final journey to the place he had selected to cease living, to stop of his own volition, the event called the Great Demise. He had attained complete mastery over his physical being and could control his own mortality. His companions as Brahmins were not allowed to eat mushrooms, but Siddhartha, knowing his own intention to cease, chose to break the dietary prohibition and ingest the tabooed mushrooms for his final meal.

Brahmins eat no beef, since the animal is sacred, and similarly all vegetative growths, like mushrooms, that spring from impure substance like the dung of cattle are forbidden. Mushrooms, as in the Selva Pasquala rock shelter, are commonly seen as a bullish zoomorphism, and cattle dung, commonly called 'cow pies,' is the common medium for the growth of *Psilocybe* mushrooms.

Mining for Golden Medicine Roots

The case of Joseph Smith, the founder of the Mormon Church of Latter Day Saints, is even more revealing of the role of entheogens in the origin of religion. His family had been caught up in the religious fervor of the bible-camps as practiced in nineteenth-century America. It is difficult, as one authority noted, to draw the line between religious ecstasy and complete nervous disorder. Accounts of their ecstatic camp meetings describe divine services where women enter such violent spasms that they strip themselves naked and jump into rivers, swooning away by the hundreds, worn out by ravings and fits, sometimes aborting from the exertions, or running on all fours and growling like animals.

The Smiths also practiced folk magic, apparently with herbal knowledge assimilated from the indigenous people. Joseph Senior and his wife experienced visions and direct communication with the Deity. The young Smith, indoctrinated by his father, began to have visions around 1820. He engaged in treasure digging, using seer stones upon which he could read or hallucinate messages. The official history of the LDS claims that this was a common practice of the day, as indeed it was, although it might seem bizarre to look for treasure buried in the primordial forest. Treasure digging was metaphoric for root doctoring. A root doctor was an herbal healer, who dug up plants looking for spiritual gold.

In 1832, the angel Mormon visited Smith and revealed the location of a buried treasure. Actually, the

Amanita muscaria as gold plates inscribed with occult letters,

senior Smith had already shown his son something similar in 1827, a stone box containing the so-called golden plates, but Junior still had certain requirements to fulfill before he was qualified to touch them. The young Smith saw in the box something like a toad, which soon assumed the appearance of a man, who struck him on the head. By 1893, as the mythologized history grew, the guardian of the treasure became an enormous toad, a flaming monster with glittering eyes.

Needless to say, the golden plates are no longer extant. Young Smith later found them for himself in a cave on the nearby Cumorah Hill, a forested drumlin where there are no caves. Drumlins are mounds of glacial deposits, forming a ridge elongated in the direction of the original ice flow, without solid rock formations capable of affording caves. Fortunately, he also found a set of magical spectacles that would allow him to read them. Like the tablets of Moses on Mount Sinai, it was a book that no one could read.

> When the mushrooms taught me the road of God and they handed over the Sacred 'Book of Knowledge,' I heard these words: 'The world is yours, you can no longer turn back.'
>
> —Juan García Carrera
> *La Otra Vida de María Sabina*

Smith, who barely had a grade-school education, was able to translate the plates miraculously with the aid of angels, from their original Egyptian, which purportedly was the language of the indigenous inhabitants of the American continent. It is not hard to conclude that the gold plates are a metaphor for something more apt to be found growing on the hill, with a toad sitting on it as its toadstool, and with a golden surface whose scabby remnants of the shattered fungal universal veil might be interpreted as an exotic language.

María Sabina similarly reported receiving a book full of wisdom from the hand of God Himself, from which she learned her songs and all her medicinal remedies. It was a book that she could not have read since she was totally illiterate. She signed her name with a thumbprint.

Smith and the early brethren routinely accessed the religious ecstasy at the divine services with a Holy Eucharist and anointing chrism that obviously was doctored with magical plants: jimsonweed, the fly-agaric toadstool, and perhaps cannabis and even peyote. The Algonquin Indian shamans of the northeast and central regions of the North American continent are known to use the two former plants in their religious ceremonies.

Smith, as a 'root-doctor,' would also have picked up traditions of voodoo magic from African-American slaves, one of whom, named Black Pete, he met in 1825, while they were both out in the woods digging for the so-called buried treasure.

Smith would also have picked up the motif of digging for hidden golden knowledge from a distant relative and member of his inner circle, Dr. Luman Walter, a physician with a reputation as a magician and mesmerist. He had traveled extensively in Europe and brought back German alchemical lore of the sacred mushroom that was the elixir of drinkable gold.

We partook together of the emblems of the body and blood of our Lord Jesus Christ and the Holy Ghost was poured out upon us in a miraculous manner. Many of our members prophesied, whilst others had the heavens opened to their view and were so overcome that we had to lay them on beds. Brother Newel saw the heaven opened and beheld the Lord Jesus Christ seated at the right hand of the Majesty on high.

—Joseph Smith
Conference of
theChurch
June 1830

God on Call

It is unbelievable that so many of Smith's congregation had such frequent and intense mystical revelations. The Eucharist routinely opened the heavens and Jesus walked among them. The dependability of the occurrence of such mystical experience by an entire congregation bears comparison with the ancient Mysteries. It is probably significant that in all the anti-Mormon rhetoric and subsequent persecutions,

Smith's brethren were not blatantly accused of taking drugs, although a deposition was made against his family as intemperate or drunkards. There was nothing illegal about a special Eucharist and it was probably a common element of 19th Century revivalist evangelism. Significantly, with the passing of the original prophetic leaders of the congregations, the heavens closed. The formula for the Eucharist and anointing chrism passed away with them.

Smith's School for Prophets, founded in 1833, is similar to the Pennsylvanian Ephrata Cloister. At the School, it was the purpose and outcome that the initiates saw Jesus Christ walking among them, causing a thrill felt through their entire body.

We, the undersigned, being personally acquainted with the family of Joseph Smith, Sr., with whom the celebrated Gold Bible, so called, originated, state: that they were not only a lazy, indolent set of men, but also intemperate.
—Neighbors of the Smith family
Mormonism Unveiled

At Ephrata, founded in 1732, a forty-day strenuous ordeal of sequestration, austerities, physical discomfort, sleep deprivation, near starvation, thirst, constant prayer, and a regime of special elixirs ended with the initiates speaking with angels. The last surviving resident of the Cloister died in 2008. Ephrata was assimilated into the German Seventh Day Baptists, who today, like all these revivalist religions, pursue a vigorous anti-drug agenda.

Similarly, the Church of Scientology, established 1953, is a science fiction assimilation of occultism, Western technology, pulp fiction, and Oriental philosophy, and has attracted many adherents with its emphasis on self-help and drug rehabilitation. Its founder claimed that the new religion was comparable to the discovery of fire. He saw a Promethean sign in his own flaming red hair. The religion condemns both psychiatry and drugs; and a group of Scientologists picketed the conference in Basel, Switzerland, which celebrated the 100th birthday of Albert Hofmann. Its slogan is: "Leading the Way to a Drug-Free World." The condemnation of psychiatry is based on the Church's belief in their more efficient procedures of electronically assisted reprogramming and indoctrination.

Despite the Church's Puritanism about drugs, its founder, L. Ron Hubbard, left a personal history of fraud, false accreditation, drug addiction, and psychotic behavior. His son signed a sworn affidavit stating: "I have personal knowledge that my father regularly used illegal drugs including amphetamines, barbiturates and hallucinogens. He regularly used cocaine, peyote, and mescaline." Others have added opium, alcohol, and a variety of prescription drugs to the list. His wife, married in bigamy, glossed this as self-medication. Hubbard died in strange circumstances, apparently from an overdose of a prescription anti-psychotic drug.

Both Old and New

Hinduism encompasses a wide variety of religious traditions in India, traceable back to the Iron Age and further back into prehistory. Soma is an essential element of the religion. Paul's toxic Eucharist is at the very earliest formation of the version of Christianity that would dominate through the Church of Rome. On the other hand, in Scientology we witness the beginning of a new religion for the 21st Century.

Despite the chorus of denials, entheogens were at the origin of religions, both the most ancient experience of the cave and of new ones forged for the interplanetary journey into the empyrean of outer space. Scientology enlists its most elite organization of the Soldiers of Light for an unending journey through the trackless galaxy. These are the origins of the religions, not the decadent phase when the lower class seeks to have a mere taste of god. Even those ministering to the problems of addiction and proselytizing an arduous pathway to the empyrean have kept secrets reserved for only the most elite.

5

CLOSED TO THE PUBLIC

Huautla de Jiménez has prospered from the visitors who want to experience where the Psychedelic Revolution began. María Sabina is honored as the priestess of the mushrooms. Her name is everywhere in the town. She herself never profited, but her descendants, who neglected her shamelessly in her old age, are eager to pursue the family business. Anyone who wishes can see the pretty pictures, but the true healing ceremony rarely occurs. The town is a viper's nest of competing shamans.

I was flying. I went very far. I could see everything illuminated all around. I went higher than the clouds, higher than everything. I realized how beautiful it is to have Light. I kept rising with the sun's rays. The higher I found myself, I realized that I was going around Señor Sun, the husband of the Moon. I remember that I made seven revolutions around our planet.

—María Sabina

Divulging Dangerous Secrets

Wasson, who was a New York banker, precipitated a profound cultural event that came to be known as the Psychedelic Revolution when he published his account of his visionary experience under the guidance of the Mazatec curandera or healer. This led to the widespread use of entheogens as recreational drugs and the colonizing of both the plant substances and the mythical realm described as the empyrean.

There's a new road now that goes to Huautla de Jiménez, the mountain village in the northernmost corner of the Mexican state of Oaxaca. When Gordon Wasson first visited in 1953, the journey took eleven hours on horseback from Teotitlán, which was the nearest town on the road system. Wasson went by the name of Gordon, R. Gordon Wasson, since his father had named both of his sons Robert after himself. On that first visit, Wasson witnessed the divinatory ritual performed by a sabio, wise man or shaman, the one-eyed butcher named Aurelio Carreras. It is strange the way that myth becomes reality, since the single eye is emblematic of the paranormal expertise that Carreras claimed to have. The predictions proved to be infallible.

On Wasson's second visit in June of 1955, he was introduced to Carreras's mother-in-law María Sabina, a shaman of formidably greater power, and he became the first outsider to participate in the nightlong vigil or velada by ingesting the visionary mushrooms, which had been kept as a carefully guarded secret rite of the Mazatec people.

Partially as publicity for his forthcoming publication of *Mushrooms, Russia, and History*, written with his wife, Valen-

Life magazine cover. May 13, 1957

At one point in the faint moonlight the bouquet on the table assumed the dimensions and shape of an imperial conveyance, a triumphal car, drawn by zoological creatures conceivable only in an imaginary mythology, bearing a woman clothed in regal splendor. The visions came in endless succession, each growing out of the preceding ones. We had the sensation that the walls of our humble house had vanished, that our untrammeled souls were floating in the empyrean, stroked by divine breeze, possessed of a divine mobility that would transport anywhere on the wings of a thought.

—R. Gordon Wasson

tina Pavlovna, Wasson published an account of the experience in the now classic 13th of May 1957 issue of the magazine Life as "Great Adventures in the Discovery of Mushrooms that Cause Strange Visions." Inadvertently, he launched what has come to be known as the Psychedelic Revolution. Within ten years, *Life* reported on LSD as a drug for psychiatric therapy that had gotten out of control. The popularizing of the mushrooms resulted in their eventual classification as a controlled or prohibited substance in the United States and elsewhere around the globe.

As a professional international banker, Wasson was a most unlikely candidate for this role. He and his wife had started writing the mushroom book in the mid-1940s as a cookbook, with merely a footnote on "the gentle art of mushroom-knowing as practiced by the northern Slavs." The footnote had grown until it replaced the book as originally planned. It was here that they had indulged their fascination in an event that dated back to their marriage in 1928, when the

Russian-born Valentina on their honeymoon in the Catskills had insisted upon gathering mushrooms, an organic growth that the Anglo-Saxon Gordon termed toadstools, and all of them without exception loathsome and poisonous. Mushrooms escape classification as a plant inasmuch as they lack chlorophyll and are either parasitic or symbiotic on other plants.

Eventually, he came to mythologize the event as Persephone's quest for the magical plant that opened up the pathways to the otherworld. In the ensuing years of investigation, as Wasson and his wife both pursued their separate careers, hers as a pediatrician, they found that their dichotomous attitude toward the mushroom was well documented in the folkloric traditions and art of Europe, leading them to suspect some deep-seated and ancient taboo against the profane use of a religious sacrament, still practiced, as they discovered, by the shamans of certain peoples of Siberia. Siberia, of course, in view of the politics of the time, was inaccessible to them, especially since the communist nation was doing its best to eradicate traces of unassimilated indigenous cultures.

> During our five-year engagement mushrooms had never come up between us and here she was possessed by mushrooms! I was beside myself. I acted the perfect Anglo-Saxon oaf confronting a wood nymph I had never before laid eyes on.
>
> —R. Gordon Wasson
> *Persephone's Quest*

Holy Children Lost their Voice

Although Wasson had tried to shield the identity of the curandera under the pseudonym of Eva Mendez, he ended up making María Sabina a 'hippie' celebrity and her village a destination for troupes of what are now called 'narco-tourists.' Inadvertently, he debased the mushrooms that once, as the Mazatecs said, "took you where God is," so that María Sabina eventually lamented that "from the moment the foreigner arrived, the holy children lost their purity, they lost their force, they ruined them; henceforth, they will no longer work; there is no remedy for it."

In the ensuing drug culture, Wasson, whose wife died in 1958, managed to remain above the fray, deploring the use of drugs for what he saw as recreational purposes, rather than spiritual enlightenment. Andrew Weil, in an article published shortly after Wasson's death in 1986, reproached him for being a snob and elitist, "relegating most of those who have experimented with sacred substances to the category of 'the Tim Learys and their ilk.'"

Wasson was fearful of contamination by association with some of the more notorious advocates of the very same aspects of the drug experience that fascinated him. Timothy Leary, for example, ate magic mushrooms in Mexico before trying LSD or any other psychoactive

> Unhappily my explanations of this sequence of personal development were often misinterpreted to mean, "Get stoned and abandon all constructive activity."
>
> —Timothy Leary

substance. This was all played out, moreover, against the backdrop of the Cold War and the interest of the United States government in competing with the Soviet Union for chemical agents for espionage and mind control. The hippie movement became inseparable from the protests against the war in Vietnam and the intergenerational gap of conservative family values and free sex.

Hofmann's Problem Child

Albert Hofmann had discovered the hallucinogenic effects of LSD on his famous bicycle ride of April 1943 and reported on it in a Swiss pharmacological journal in 1947. The US government had already been in competition with the Nazis in the search for a truth serum or drug, but the agency involved was disbanded upon the completion of the war, whereupon, however, the Nazi experiments with mescaline in the Dachau concentration camp were uncovered, causing the US to begin mescaline studies of its own. By the time news of LSD finally appeared in the *American Psychiatric Journal* in 1950, the US was already engaged in covert experiments. And by 1951, the quixotic charismatic super-spy and entrepreneur Captain Al Hubbard, the so-called 'Johnny Appleseed of LSD,' was turning on thousands of people, including scientists, and some of the most well-placed politicians, intelligence officials, diplomats, and church figures.

Wasson emerged as the authority whose validation was sought by others in the field, and he found himself embarrassingly linked in a triumvirate with Timothy Leary, whose proselytizing he considered naïve and reckless, leading to a life as an outlaw, and Carlos Castaneda, whose *Teachings of Don Juan*, published in 1966, was even more influential in popularizing the paranormal aspects of the psychedelic experience. Castaneda is now debunked as somewhat of a phony, although the fictionalized account of his Yaqui shaman is a composite of largely authentic phenomena.

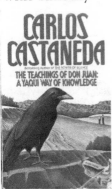

Teachings of Don Juan
by Carlos Castaneda,

Soma
by R. Gordon Wasson

Divine Mushroom of Immortality

In 1963, Wasson retired from banking, and on the afternoon of the very day, he boarded a merchant ship for the Orient to gather material there that he would publish in 1968, *Soma: Divine Mushroom of Immortality*. In Soma, he sought the origin of the European mycophobia— a term he coined for the inordinate dread of mushrooms, tracing it back to the importation of an Indo-European mushroom cult, documented among the ancient Aryans. He identified their Vedic plant-god Soma as *Amanita muscaria*. From 1965, when he returned from the Far East, until his death, he lived comfortably in Connecticut at his Danbury estate, presiding as the patrician over the controversy caused by his Soma identification and seeking still further confirmation of its validity.

Sacred Mushroom and the Cross

When that validation came in the form of John Allegro's *Sacred Mushroom and the Cross*, published in 1970, he didn't recognize it, much to Allegro's disappointment. Allegro, the linguist and scholar of the Dead Sea Scrolls, an academic with impeccable credentials in ancient Classical and Near and Middle Eastern languages, had already published several books. He had read Wasson's writings and appropriately acknowledged them, knew of his Mexican discoveries, accepted his identification of Soma as the fly-agaric, and obviously had drawn the conclusion that Wasson was still reluctant to make.

However, as an amateur scholar, Wasson always deferred to the opinion of professionals. Allegro's linguistic argument was beyond Wasson's expertise; Wasson was proficient only in French and Spanish. He reportedly gave the book only a cursory examination, and, despite his cultural openness, he would have found the sexual obsession of the fertility cults of the goddess excessive, an opinion shared by many readers. As was his wont, he sought the opinion of two respected friends, a Jewish rabbi and a Catholic monsignor, who assured him that "there was not one single word of truth in the book whatsoever." This was actually a disappointment, since he and Valentina had always suspected that there might have been a mushroom cult in Christianity, which would have been the closer and more obvious reason for the European mycophobia, rather than the archetype of a remembrance from the most distant past. Too late, just before his death, he came to change his rejection of the role of a sacramental fruit in the biblical account of Eden.

Wasson wrote that he was 'ready for the storm' for his personally intimidating, yet exhilarating admission, but there was no storm. Nobody cared. Allegro's book had elicited two full-length rebuttals, rushed into print within a year of his publication. Recently, a lavishly

> I once said that there was no mushroom in the Bible. I was wrong. It plays a hidden role (that is, hidden from us until now) and a major one, in what is the best known episode in the Old Testament, the Garden of Eden story and what happened to Adam and Eve.
>
> —R. Gordon Wasson
> *Persephone's Quest*

I had always had a horror of those who preached a kind of pseudo-religion of telepathy, who for me were unreliable people, and if our discoveries in Mexico were to be drawn to their attention we were in danger of being adopted by such undesirables.

—R. Gordon Wasson
Persephone's Quest

illustrated survey of the Dead Sea Scrolls displays a few photographs of Allegro at work, but not a single mention of the Allegro scandal.

Door of Eternity

Wasson similarly shied away from Andrija Puharich's investigation into the paranormal aspects of the experience accessed through the visionary mushrooms, even though Wasson had personally affirmed the validity of the entheogen as an agent for clairvoyance and astral projection in an experiment they had arranged. Other members of Wasson's expedition into the Oaxaca highlands reported similar paranormal experiences. All these events were induced by the Mexican mushrooms, which were *Psilocybes*, whose psychoactive effect had previously been unknown to outsiders.

Wasson had first met Puharich through Alice Boverie, a New York socialite, who had learned of Gordon and Valentina's ongoing research for their *Russia, Mushrooms, and History* from a reference librarian at the Public Library, while investigating psychoactive mushrooms. Puharich, an American-born medical doctor and parapsychologist of Croatian descent, at the time was a captain with the United States Army, stationed at the Fort Detrick Chemical and Biological Warfare Center in Edgewood, Maryland, working for the CIA on chemical and other means of mind control. With Wasson's permission, he dutifully passed on the information about Aurelio Carreras to his military associates. As a result, a CIA mole, James Moore, infiltrated Wasson's 1956 expedition to Mexico, funded with a generous financial grant, clearly indicating that the intelligence community regarded a divinatory mushroom as a valuable tool in their arsenal. Moore found the journey extremely unpleasant, and although he witnessed the séance, he was extremely ill. Eight kilos thinner, he fled with a packet of the mushrooms, intending to isolate and synthesize the chemical, which, in fact, Albert Hofmann succeeded in doing before him. The French mycologist Roger Hiem identified them as *Psilocybe caerulescens* and the psychoactive agent was named 'psilocybin'.

However, it was a strange event involving the *Amanita muscaria* that had led Boverie to seek out Wasson. She was a psychic or 'channeler.' She had unwittingly precipitated a bizarre psychic seizure in June of 1954 when she handed an ancient Egyptian cartouche to Harry Stone, a visiting Dutch sculptor. Although he knew neither the Egyptian language nor its art, he became possessed by a persona that they later identified as Rahótep—pronounced Ra ho Tep, a man who had lived 4600 years ago. In the course of similar occurrences over the next three years, Harry spoke Egyptian, wrote hieroglyphics, and disclosed the role of *Amanita* in Egyptian cult and divination.

The Sacred Mushroom: Key to the Door of Eternity

Puharich offered an account of the whole affair in his *The Sacred Mushroom: Key to the Door of Eternity*, published in 1959. Although Wasson maintained cordial relations with Puharich, and Puharich in 1961 gave him a copy of his laboratory experiment showing significant improvement in telepathy with subjects who had ingested *Amanita muscaria*, Wasson cautioned him about the pejorative notoriety that might result from the Associated Press release about his ESP experiments, although it was just such notoriety that the *Life* magazine article had secured for himself.

Colonizing the Empyrean

There were two sides to the Psychedelic Revolution: the liberals seeking entheogens to free the psyche and the conservatives seeking to control the mind by using the same substances as drugs. The abuses and excesses of both led to the Controlled Substances Act of 1970. As indignant parents continued to agitate to place yet another substance on the prohibited list, the revolution also fueled intense interest in mythology and comparative religion, as those same hippies who now are parents sought guidance for understanding their experiences, propelling books like Joseph Campbell's *Hero with a Thousand Faces* into best sellers.

Today, the chemical industry is ransacking the cultural heritage

Dear Mr. Steve Jobs,
    Hello from Albert Hofmann. I understand from media accounts that you feel LSD helped you creatively in your development of Apple computers and your personal spiritual quest. I'm interested in learning more about how LSD was useful to you.

—Written shortly after Hofmann's 101st birthday

of the indigenous peoples of the Amazonian forests for new botanicals, whose constituent agents can be isolated and manufactured, and thereby sold at considerable profit, while even greater profit is generated by the illegal commerce in drugs for recreational use. The empyrean has been commercialized and sacred plants reduced to chemicals, have lost their efficacy as entheogens. Indigenous healers, whose secrets are stolen at the same time that the habitat of the native plants is being deforested, repeat María Sabina's lament. The outsiders see the pretty pictures, but few are willing, as we will see, to follow the rigorous and physically debilitating diet of plants that can access the true shamanic potential.

Herbal lore of Europe has been secularized. The special rituals for enlisting the spirit resident in the entheogen were labeled as superstition and relegated to pagan witchcraft, even though most plants in the ancient medical compendia have mythical names. As early as the arrival of the priests who accompanied the Conquistadors and the wave of immigration, the healing plants of the indigenous peoples were gathered and classified with proper Linnaean nomenclature. The lore was colonized. The chants that are sung to the spirits in the plants are preserved separately in ethnographic compilations. The chemicals without the resident deity and the ministering shaman lose their voice. They no longer speak. They no longer heal. Cosmic consciousness is now a party drug.

> Our normal waking consciousness, rational consciousness, as we call it, is but one especial type of consciousness, whilst all about it, parted from it by the filmiest of screens, there lie potential forms of consciousness entirely different.
>
> —William James
> *Varieties of Religious Experience*

In the same way, various religions have colonized the
empyrean—staked out a territorial claim, offering exclu-
sive access only to their membership, or even more bold-
ly, they have equated it totally with their monotheistic
deity. The Psychedelic Revolution sent many of the most
creative minds, either physically or spiritually, to the
Orient in search for meaning in a religion that defines
the territory not as a deity, but as accessible through the
guidance of a great teacher. In Europe and elsewhere, the
religions of paganism or animism similarly decolonized
the realm through polytheistic diversity, where god is
seen as one of many modes of channeling the numinous
into an array of intercessory configurations, a plurality of
numinous entities.

Entheogen Dilemma

The dilemma of the entheogen, separating toxin from
the spirit, is portrayed in the mythical narrative of the
hero Philoctetes. He is the man who inherited the poisoned bow and arrows of Heracles when the great hero
left this world. Philoctetes took part in the Trojan War,
but as the expedition approached the enemy shore, a
serpent bit him. The toxins induced uncontrollable
spasms of ecstasy and caused his foot to turn gangre-
nous. His fellow soldiers could not stand the trances,
the shouting, and the noisome stench. So they abandoned him. Toward the end of the long-drawn-out war,
they learned that they would never take Troy without
their rejected comrade. So they sent a contingent of
soldiers to steal his bow. Only at the last moment, they
realized that the toxins of the bow would be worthless
without the bowman. With Philoctetes and his bow,
they took Troy, and the bowman was healed of his
toxins.

6

Strange People

Entheogens suggest the manner of their anthropomorphic or zoomorphic visualization. Mythology has a broad catalogue of creatures that materialize as companions for the psychoactive journey. The journey is not solely the result of expectation or indoctrination. Entheogens have a say in the matter. The plant has a program of its own.

Mind of its Own

An entheogen may appear as a 'little soul guide'. In the case of the African iboga, he takes you by the hand in the therapy session, like Marley's ghost, to view the errors of your past. Visions in the indigenous Bwiti initiatory context are further determined by intense ritual preparation in a temple environment with topographical symbolism. After the ceremony, the candidates are quizzed as to the nature of the visions. If they are not the correct ones, the ceremony will have to be repeated. The initiates see a procession of dead ancestors, withered and white as ghosts.

People who have taken some of the psychedelic mushrooms that were used in Middle America have told me that they begin to have images that resemble those of the Aztec gods. Certain psychedelics produce images of this type; others produce images of another type.
—Joseph Campbell
The Hero's Journey

Mother Salvia

Salvia divinorum commonly materializes as a female, *la hembra*, both to the indigenous Mazatec shamans and even to outsiders. The lady is Mother Salvia. She is dubbed 'Sally,' shy and modest and speaks with a quiet voice. She has been assimilated to Christianity as the Virgin Mary, but identified as a shepherdess, *la pastora*. This is not an attribute of the Virgin and indicates a Pre-Conquest persona. She appears wise and imparts knowledge for personal growth, but also can be angered if consumed without due reverence or when combined trivially with other intoxicants beneath her status.

Traditionally, due respect requires abstinence from sex and alcohol for a period of days both before and after the consultation. The preparatory abstinence may make chemical sense, but reportedly infringing upon the ban within the proscribed period after the experience, even just with sex, can have dire consequences. This cannot be explained rationally as a side effect of any medicine.

There are several candidates for salvia's Aztec name. One is called 'the noble prince,' pipilzintzintli. Such a title obviously implies an honorific anthropomorphism. Often Mazatec shamans do employ other plants with the lady and these materialize as members of her family: the 'male,' the 'child,' and the 'godson.'

> After only a few minutes I feel my friend Iboga come back and say, "We're really not through yet. I have many more things to say." Then the face of this black man in his 50s with a brown beard, brown thick coat and a staff kept appearing to me. I didn't understand a word; it might not have been English.
>
> —Patient using ibogaine for addictive relief

Ayahuasca

With *ayahuasca*, the visions are most often of serpents, pumas, and jaguars, even in an urban setting and for people alien to Amazonia. The anthropologist Michael Harner reports that giant reptilian creatures material-ized to him, complete with a mythological scenario of their identity as extraterrestrials, who came to earth to escape an enemy in outer space from whom they have hidden, disguised within multitudinous animal and botanical life forms on this planet.

Similarly, Gerardo Reichel-Dolmatoff reports that the Desana indigenous tribesmen of the Amazon ba-sin trace descent from ancestors who arrived in canoes shaped like huge serpents; and they depict the human brain with two snakes lodged between the two hemi-spheres. These serpents symbolize the male and female principle, like the caduceus of Hermes; and more broadly, these serpents can be any oppositional binary dichotomy, which must be mediated to achieve individual awareness. The serpents are imagined as spiraling rhythmically in a swaying motion from side to side.

Commonly DMT—the visionary chemical in the *ayahuasca* potion—materializes as a per-sonified inner voice or other, who is a transper-sonal guide toward total fulfillment or whole-ness. Adepts dub it the 'DMT elf,' a gnome-like, playful and usually friendly creature. These elves can multiply into

On the basis of first-hand experience—both my own and that of persons who were with me in sessions—I can testify that the seeing of felines also occurs in urban con-texts which are distinctly non-Amazonian.

—Benny Shanon
The Antipodes of the Mind:

groups of little dancing beings. Often the guides take on the guise of little insect-headed aliens, *homunculi*, perhaps from outer space. Such extraterrestrial fantasies are a component in the theology of Scientology.

Occurrence of these little creatures or of specific shamanic animal familiars may be influenced by expectation. An African plant should have an African guide; or an Amazonian plant, an animal powerful in the indigenous shamanism of the jungle; but people who experience them seem to feel there is more to it than that. Albert Hofmann self-experimented with the *Psilocybe mexicana* mushroom, knowing full well their Mexican origin, but try as he might, he could not escape an Aztec scenario for his experience, complete with a vision of himself about to be sacrificed by the priest.

Onset of the visionary state is often heralded by brain-stimulated geometric imagery, entopic visualizations arising from the human anatomical optical system itself, in which the eye is viewing the flow of blood in the retina and visual cortex. These designs or frets are called grecas because they occur on Greek vases, probably as an indication of visionary experience, but they predate Greek civilization, going back to the 5th millennium BCE. Cave paintings sometimes draw the frets within the body of human figures, so that the greca becomes an anthropomorphized hallucination. A beautiful Mayan exemplar represents the figure of a 'humanized labyrinth',

Labyrinth Humanoid

which probably served as a focus for intense meditation and visualization in an initiatory ceremony.

Voice of the Plant

Shamans claim that they can communicate with the indwelling spirit of animate plants or entheogens. According to them, that is how they discovered that a plant with DMT must be combined with another that supplies the MAOI inhibitor. There are a variety of such plants, but they do not grow naturally together and there is nothing about their physical appearance that might suggest combining them. Discovery through trial and error is unlikely. María Sabina discovered the mushrooms by herself at the age of seven while tending goats, with no instruction from her mother and totally without knowledge of their role in Mazatec shamanism. Her mother had made a conscious effort not to tell her about the mushrooms since she thought that her daughter was too clever and would get into trouble. If the plants have a specific language that speaks to the inspired herbalist, it is probable that the animate plant's spirit or its indwelling deity also has a typical appearance.

Some initiation candidates report see-

María Sabina, age 7, discovering mushrooms

One morning, as was my custom to accompany the goats in the field, one of them got away from the rest. I had to go after it. It was then that I discovered the mushrooms, like hard flowers. I decided to put them in my mouth so as not to have any doubts about them.... [She shared them with her sister.] Those little things made us feel good; we sang, we danced, and we whistled, and later we cried.

—Juan García Carrera
La Otra Vida de María Sabina

ing the ultimate basis of life, the double helix of the
DNA, intertwined as two serpents. As we have mentioned, this has been stylized since Classical antiquity
as the caduceus of the messenger god Hermes. It is an
emblem with strong entheogenic significance since it
symbolizes both the medicinal toxins and the ability
to travel between worlds. Such a trip may even imply
the alternation of sexual identity. Shamanic initiation
is often experienced as accessing the opposite sexual
persona, commemorated by the acquisition of a corresponding suit of clothing. The illiterate María Sabina
in her shamanic chant declared that she had balls and
was learned like a lawyer.

Shamans talk with plants and animals, with all of nature. This is not just a metaphor. They do it in an altered state of consciousness. In the Amazon, shamans know the various plants and the songs that go with the plants, which they commonly learn from the plants themselves.

—Michael Harner
The Way of the Shaman

The vision of the
DNA is comparable
to Dmitri Mendeleev's
discovery of the periodic
table of the elements in
a daytime moment of
dreaming while playing
something like solitaire
with a modified deck of
cards representing the
elements and listening
to chamber music being
played in the adjacent
room. The music aided
him to slip into a trance state of lucid dreaming, in
which the musical scale suggested the arrangement of
the elements into octaves. This basic pattern can be
traced back to the Greek Pythagoras, who envisioned it
while listening to the hammering of a blacksmith. The
music of the blacksmith is probably a motif of mythologized history, like the role of the blacksmith in the last
meal of the Buddha, and suggests the alchemical theme

of the volcanic crucible. Mendeleev was a founding member of the Physical Society and dabbled in spiritualism and mysticism, investigating whether it had any scientific basis. Earlier in the 1860s, the English chemist John Newland had proposed a similar arrangement of the elements as octaves, but the Royal Chemical Society rejected the idea as Pythagorean mysticism.

Mendeleev was the grandson of an Orthodox priest, and as a chemist, he was continuing in the science that was still called alchemy in the previous century. His mother ran a glass factory after the death of his father. The glass foundry was an essential industry for manufacturing the vessels used in alchemy. The Periodic Chart actually demonstrates how lead could be transmuted into gold, but with such a tremendous expenditure of energy that the transformation would be economically unfeasible.

Alchemy had an obsession with numbers, and God was seen as the divine geometer in creating the perfection of the cosmos and of man in His image. The mystical significance of the Pythagorean octave had passed into Christian traditions. As the only cubed number—2x2x2—of the decade, eight suggested the Trinity. There were eight days between Christ's entrance into Jerusalem on the ass and the Resurrection; and by the magical technique of gematria, where every letter is assigned a numerical value, the name of Jesus yielded 888, which is to say a trinity of eights. The octagon is the traditional shape of the baptismal fount and of the baptistery. In early Christianity, baptism was experienced as a psychoactive transcendence, reflected in the spiraling design of the traditional baptistery.

In early Christianity, baptism was experienced as a psychoactive transcendence.

The octave is the essential pattern of DNA, which transmits the molecular information governing life and evolution as 64 bits of code, which is to say, the square of eight. The same pattern has been influential in other fields. The Croatian electrical engineer Nikola Tesla invented the generator of alternating current after a series of visions where he saw that the cosmos obeyed the law of octaves. The architect Buckminster Fuller developed the geodesic dome based on the 'co-ordinate system of the universe', specifically on the octaves of Mendeleev's Periodic Chart. Interestingly, Timothy Leary, unaware of the precedents, applied his theory of the eight circuits of the nervous system to his space-age interpretation of Gnostic revelation.

Dwarfism and Gigantism

Some entheogens, like the *Amanita muscaria*, induce oscillating alterations in the perception of size: micropsia and macropsia, seeing things too small or too big. The latter can give one the impression of suddenly flying closer to a distant object.

This phenomenon was popularized in Lewis Carroll's description of Alice's encounter with the blue caterpillar in Wonderland sitting atop a mushroom, smoking his cannabis hookah. He tells her that one side of the mushroom will make her shrink smaller, the other grow taller. Wonderland is peopled with a menagerie of helpful or disturbing anthropomorphic creatures, and the entire scenario is an adventure of self-discovery through an underworld journey. It is probable that the author modeled the whole tale on ancient religious mystery initiations to please Alice's father, who was a renowned Classical scholar.

In the myth of the hero Hercules' encounter with the pygmies, he was so exhausted after his battle with the giant Antaeus that he fell asleep. When he awoke, the little creatures that were the brothers of the giant had tied him down. This is the source of Jonathan Swift's account of Gulliver and the Lilliputians. The giant Antaeus is the model for Swift's Brobdingnagians. The original title of the work was *Travels into Several Remote Nations*.

Caterpillar using a hookah and seated on a mushroom in *Alice in Wonderland*

Fingerlings

Later ancient writers identified the pygmies with the short Ethiopian tribesmen, making them the length of a forearm or pygmé, but the pygmé is also a fist and the creatures of myth were much smaller, only as big as the fingers of such a fist. Hercules had apparently fallen into a drunken trance, since the little creatures used ladders to climb up into his drinking cup, and they were so small that they used needles for spears. Their relationship to their brother the giant implies that the whole heroic exploit was another instance of Hercules on a drug trip, encountering the guides who materialized as the size-shifting anthropomorphized mushroom.

Antaeus derived his power from contact with the earth. The only way to defeat him was to lift him up and hold him away until he withered like a plant. The early 1600 folktale of Tom Thumb is an indication of the longevity of these fingerlings. A hundred years later, Henry Fielding made him the hero of a tragical *History of Tom Thumb the Great*.

These mythical miniscule pygmies were the soul guides in various ancient religious mystery initiations. They were depicted as playful creatures, definitely not the length of a forearm, and characterized by their enormous erections, with the penis as the equivalent for an additional leg or foot. Another name for them was dactyls or 'finger-men.' The 'finger' is a common euphemism for the penis, as are also the 'leg' and the 'foot,' so that the Old Testament even refers to urine euphemistically as 'foot water.' Traditionally, the tiny creatures materialized in pentads, groups of five, like the digits of the pygmé or fist. Their relationship to their brother the giant implies the fantasized gigantism of the aroused penis, as well as the perceptual dualism of the drug-induced experience and the magical alternation in the size of the penis.

The dwarf of the Mayan Uxmal pyramid complex is a version of the great plumed serpent Quetzalcoatl, and both are materialized from the *Amanita muscaria*. The divine

> To one who has eaten them, the little saints appear as tiny beings the size of playing card kings. The sacred mushrooms, when consumed under the proper circumstances and in the right number, put one in a trance whereupon little men known as *los Señores* emerge and deal with the problems that concern you.
>
> —R. Gordon Wasson
> *The Wondrous Mushroom*

serpent was also a bird, and laid an egg from which the dwarf hatched. His foster mother was a shaman and found and tended the egg. It was this dwarf who built the Pyramid of the Diviner at Uxmal.

The Greek heroes themselves were portrayed as dwarfish black pygmies on the enormous double-handled drinking cups employed for administering the entheogenic potion for certain of these mystery initiations. This means that the hero or initiate became consubstantial with the toxic plant or plants that materialized as the pygmies.

Similar pentads or groups of five are the corybants, named as little helmeted dancers. They first materialized from the fingers of the earth goddess as she grabbed the ground in labor. They were interchangeable with another group called 'boys' or kuretes. They danced ecstatically around her and clashed their spears to hide the cries of her newborn infant. As dancers characterized by their dome-shaped helmet, they, too, are personified mushrooms, lascivious and equally phallic, like the little finger-men. They also were guides in mystery initiations.

There was an old woman who lived in a hut. She went mourning that she had no children. In her distress, she one day took an egg, covered it with a cloth, and laid it away carefully in one corner of her hut. Every day she went to look at it, until one morning she found the egg hatched and a creature or baby born. In one year it walked and talked like a man; and then it stopped growing. The old woman was more delighted than ever, and said he would be a great lord or king.

—John Lloyd Stephens
Incidents of Travel in Central America

Bes says, "Make me a temple just a forearm high!" The deceased says, "Are you not a giant seven times taller? How could you enter a temple so small, but that is what you did."

—Egyptian Pyramid Text

Like all of these creatures, they were associated with the netherworld volcanic forge of the god Hephaestus/Vulcan, whose metallurgical expertise implies the art of spiritual transmutation later known as alchemy. They were often interchangeable with the Cabiri, who were originally from Egypt, little penis men, better known as Bes, the creator god, a favorite of the ladies' bed, a squat knock-kneed dwarf, bearded with a swollen head and prominent genitals. These tiny creatures were known as the Great Gods.

7

COURT DWARFS

The Greeks named the Pygmies of Ethiopia after the little people who already existed in the realm of myth. The bandy-legged dwarf was a divinity who incarnated the most primordial and elemental powers of Nature, a kind of Great Spirit, older than the separation of the divine into more or less unified and coherent pantheons. The gods of those most primordial times have as one of their characteristics the ability to materialize as dwarfs. When an actual pygmy was discovered, he fell into the magical paradigm and was considered a being with all the power of an entheogenic guide. Dwarves continued to be a favorite in the courts of Europe and Turkey. The famous dwarf

Come home immediately. Hurry and bring with you this pygmy that you have taken alive, healthy, and unharmed from the country of the people of the East, for the dances of the gods, to gladden the heart, to delight the heart of the Pharaoh. When he boards the boat with you, see to it that there are able-bodied men around him for protection, to keep him from falling into the water. When he sleeps at night, see to it that able-bodied men sleep around him in his tent. Go to check on him ten times each night. My Majesty desires to see this pygmy more than the produce from the land of the mines.

—Letter from Pharaoh Pepi II
On discovering a living pygmy

of Queen Henrietta Maria was reportedly an implausible
eighteen inches tall.

Shade-foots

The traditions of Classical antiquity have a menagerie
of such little creatures that materialized from the land
of myth with attributes of the mushroom guide. Pride
of place belongs to the Shade-foots or One-foots. They
are a tribe native to India with but a single foot and a
leg of extraordinary agility. They leap up vigorously,
and when they tire, they fall on their backs to rest in
the shade cast by their foot that is the size of sunshade.
Their likeness to an anthropomorphized mushroom is
obvious, and their Indian habitat identifies them as the
Vedic Aja Ekapad, the 'Not born Single-foot,' one of
the epithets of the intoxicating plant god, Soma.

The attribute of not being born refers to the apparently seedless appearance of the mushroom as it bursts
suddenly from the ground, thrust up by its powerful leg.
Siberian tribesmen inebriated with the *Amanita muscaria* imitate this characteristic, as they jump up and
down, even pushing their heads through restraining
membranes. The dancing leg is like the depiction of the
mushroom-men in the rock-shelter Neolithic painting
of the Selva Pasquala.

Through him who is the Heart
    of Heaven, One-leg by
name. One-Leg Lightning-bolt
is the first. And second is Dwarf
      Lightning-bolt.

—Popol Vuh
On Huracan
The mushroom creator god

Shade-foots
were first men-
tioned in Aristo-
phanes' comic par-
ody of a mystery
initiation in the
Clouds, along with
other similar crea-

tures, which leaves little doubt that they were all well known to the ancient audience as anthropomorphisms of the initiatory fungal plant guide. The same materialization is documented for Mesoamerican shamanism, and depicted as such in some of the Mayan mushroom-stones. The shade of the Greek creatures that forms their foot is an umbrella or sunshade, but a shade is also a ghost or spirit. The others in Aristophanes' troupe were the One-Eyes—Monophthalmoi, who were called Arimaspians in their Scythian language. An ancient poet reported

> She saw in a moment why they had looked like mushrooms. They had been lying flat on their backs, each with its single leg straight up in the air and its enormous foot spread out above it.
>
> —C.S. Lewis
> *Voyage of the Dawn Treader*

seeing them on his ecstatic trip. They were often engaged in battle with the griffins that guarded the gateway to the gold in the netherworld. The griffin was a monstrous hybrid composed of a winged lion with the head of an eagle, often with a mushroom growing from its beak. The griffins are not difficult to recognize as shamanic familiars, guarding the pathway of the one-eyed guides. The single eye, as we have shown, is emblematic of altered vision.

Orb-eyes

One-Eyes are a version of the Orb-Eyes or Cyclopes, like the dwarfish henchmen at the alchemical forge of the god Hephaestus. The fungal anthropomorphism is explicitly portrayed on the large ceramic burial vase or urn from the mystery religion enacted at the ancient Greek sanctuary of Eleusis. The neck of the gigantic

I once wrote that the bemush-roomed person is poised in space, a disembodied eye, invisible, incorporeal, seeing but not seen.

—R. Gordon Wasson
Road to Eleusis

amphora depicts the episode where Odysseus plunges the burning timber into the single eye of the drunken Cyclops Polyphemus. As the eye sizzles, it drops a single tear in the shape of a mushroom. The area around the figures is decorated with the entopic visionary frets or grecas. The use of the amphora as a burial urn is significant since it might be expected to incorporate mythical motifs related to the Mystery initiation and the terminal life journey. The sacred road to the Eleusinian sanctuary was lined with such funeral monuments. On the body of the vase, Perseus is harvesting the head of the Gorgon Medusa, who is the most enduring anthropomorphism of the sacred mushroom. This scene also incorporates grecas, and the Gorgons are represented with cauldrons for heads. Traditionally, art historians have seen no relationship between the two themes depicted on this vase.

Hats and Helmets

Along with the Shade-foots and the One-Eyes in Aristophanes' parody are another people called the Tongue-in-Bellies or Englottogasteres. Their version of the anthropomorphism consists in converting the cap of the mushroom into the creature's upper body, so that it has only a head supported by its leg. Naming the top of the mushroom its 'cap' commonly implies this, as if a hat sat atop a creature wearing it. This is inescapable even in botanical nomenclature where it is called the *pileus*, which is Latin for 'cap.' It is not simply a cap, however; it is a skullcap, often used also to refer to the Phrygian cap, associated with Mithraism and with manumission of slaves or liberty.

In this latter significance, it was used to name the liberty-cap mushroom, a species of *Psilocybe*. The pileus was frequently worn under a

Mithras, wearing the Phrygian cap, tauroctony.

helmet, and the helmet was of the same shape, like the ones worn by the helmeted corybantic dancers. Not infrequently, the initiatory entheogen is employed in sub-visionary dosages for warriors on the battlefield. Heavier dosages would be involved in the visionary experience of initiatory induction to the military fraternity, as in Mithraism and the Nordic berserkers.

In the ranks of these little creatures were also the Cover-Mushrooms—*Kaulomyketes*. Here we have the truth revealed that they were actually 'mushrooms' or *mykes*, but they materialized as little warriors, whose shield was the cap, and they used their stem or stipe as a spear.

Zoomorphic Anthropoids

These ecstatic creatures of the wilderness were given fuller materializations in Classical mythology as hybrids of humans and various animals or plants. Satyrs or goat-men are the personification of the divine possession experienced by the bacchants or *maenads*. These goat-men represent the wild botanical antecedents of the

Tezcatlipoca, brother of the beneficent Quetzalcoatl, epitomizes conflict and instability throughout the universe. His name means Smoking Mirror, and he is commonly represented with an obsidian disk positioned at the back of his head and another replacing one of his feet—a prosthesis that locates him within the realms of both worlds: the upper world of light and life, and the lower world of darkness and death. The smokiness of his mirror alludes to the fog enshrouded nature of the images he reflects.

—Blaise D. Staples
Graeco-Roman Ruins in the New World

god, before he came to be identified with wine and the art of viticulture. In addition to their prominent ithyphallic attribute, they had some equine characteristics. The horse zoomorphism is more pronounced in the silens, to whom they are very similar.

The satyrs and silens differ from the centaurs, whose entire lower body is that of a horse. The association of the former with intoxication is obvious because of their involvement with the god Dionysus/Bacchus. The centaurs are similarly mediators with the realm of the entheogens in that they are notorious drunkards and also teach young heroes the art of archery. The bow and arrow, as we have seen, implies the whole metaphoric complex of intoxication.

The botanical essence of various trees, moreover, could also be anthropomorphized as females in the form of caryatids—a nut tree, dryads—oak tree, hamadryads —eight, each of a different tree, and so on. Their male equivalents are creatures of the woodland like the goatman Pan or the fauns, but they are largely interchangeable with satyrs. Faunus, however, was a handsome young male and could have the legs, smooth-skinned

body, and tail of a deer; hence, 'fawn' in English for a
year-old deer. The deer attributes obviously associate
him with the Siberian shamanism and the *Amanita
muscaria.*

Both Pan and Faunus played the syrinx or panpipes.
This musical instrument, like a harmonica composed of
hollow reeds, implicates them in the botanical complex
of an entheogen and ecstatic possession since Syrinx
was a maiden, like Apollo's Daphne, who was metamorphosed into the hollow water reeds from which the panpipe is made in order to escape an amorous encounter
with Pan. It was reportedly water maidens who rescued
her in this fashion; hence they are probably versions of
the mermaid, and ultimately of the primordial mermaid,
the Gorgon Medusa. A version of Pan, in fact, was a
goat-fish, who became the constellation Capricorn.
Both Pan and Faunus could be multiplied into a whole
host of identical creatures of the woodland.

The haunting music of the panpipe was thought to
induce a transcendent trance. Pan's psychoactive nature
is preserved in the word
'panic.' Sometimes the
double flute is substituted
for the panpipe. The flute
brings us back to the Gor-
gon Medusa since it was supposed to reproduce sound
the of the rasping hissing of the serpents that formed
her *chevelure.* The double flute, which was voiced by
vibrating reeds like the oboe, was supposed to induce
lascivious sexuality.

> The haunting music
> of the panpipe was
> thought to induce a
> transcendent trance.

Fortunately, since Athena made the Medusa into
a hideous monster, men are reluctant to engage with
her, although she really is surpassingly beautiful and
voluptuous. Both the panpipe and the double flute—*au-*

los—are musical instruments that serve as surrogates for a mind-altering entheogen. The same is true of Apollo's lyre —*phorminx*, which is an instrument like a kithara). The stretchers for the strings are cow/bull horns, and the plucking of the strings imitates the twanging of the bow with its toxic arrows, but instead of causing death, the sound plunges the entire universe into a transcendent musical enchantment.

Although Pan is probably etymologically derived from the verb 'to pasture,' as in his role as a herdsman, it could also suggest the 'All' that is the totality of being. Hence, there were traditions that claimed he was the child of the empyreal ether, encoded in the mystical dictum that 'All is one,' *pan to hen*.

Wee Folk

The little creatures are known as the wee folk in Celtic lore. The most generic name is fairy, derived from Latin *fata*, as a 'fate' deity. The *fata* are etymologically what has been 'said.' This implies a foretelling of the ultimate journey to the realm of the dead, with connotations of inspired speech, ecstasy, and madness. Their identity as anthropomorphisms of the mushroom is a commonplace in the tales told of them. To their ranks belongs the whole troupe of creatures like gnomes, pucks, elves, trolls, leprechauns, and the like. They, too, are commonly depicted in folk art as fungal anthropomorphisms, usually with the red cap spotted with white characteristic of the *Amanita muscaria*.

Fairy Fare

Inevitably, since they are anthropomorphisms of the entheogen, they are associated with special tables. In addition to their mushroom tables spread with dainty morsels, they were said to leave round cakes or breads of barley or oatmeal about on the ground, but the food was cursed and should never be eaten except in times of the severest hunger. The scabby white remnants of the Amanita's universal veil that shatters as the cap fully expands to the likeness of a tabletop immediately suggest the bits of forbidden food with which it is spread. A similar taboo lurks in the naming of the mushroom as a loathsome toadstool. Fairies are notorious for kidnapping people away to their realm, in a rapture possessed by a fairy wind. Conversely, a piece of bread was the surest amulet to ward off a blast of the dangerous kidnapping fairy wind.

> A little mushroom table spread,
> After short prayers, they set on bread.
>
> —Robert Herrick
> Oberon's feast
> in Hesperides

In Classical myth, the fairy table occurs as the tables desecrated by the droppings of the 'raptors' or bird-women called Harpies, who similarly were thought to materialize in a whirlwind to snatch someone suddenly away to the other realm.

> Upon a mushroom's head, Our table we do spread.
>
> —Queen Mab's Invitation

8

Confronting Self

Various tales told of the hero are composed of recurrent motifs, contrasting the self and its reflected image. The role of the entheogen is essential in bringing the two personae into an alliance. This reconciliation is the fundamental objective of psychotherapy. Myth provides a pathway for self-discovery.

The Face in the Mirror

Weird folk who materialize from the entheogen and act as guides are not the strangest creatures you encounter on a trip. The strangest encounter is with yourself.

Myth provides a pathway for self-discovery. The mirror casts back a beguiling likeness where everything is reversed. Narcissus was so entranced with his reflected image that he fell into a 'narcosis', which is a word derived from the psychoactive narkissos flower. He never returned, but plunged down through the watery reflection into the world beyond. Some claimed that it was actually his sister he saw, a twin—his opposite.

Lewis Carroll's sequel to *Alice in Wonderland*, *Through the Looking Glass and What Alice Found There*, popularized a divining technique of the 19th Century elite. Advances in the manufacture of mirrors had made it possible to produce full wall-sized mirrors. Such a mirror could be installed behind a blank door. Guests,

suitably medicated with opiate tinctures, could hallucinate upon their own assembled party reflected in the
opened doorframe.

In the paradigmatic myth of the hero, this reflected
image or alternate persona represents all the attributes
rejected in the defining of the self, a being composed of
all the opposite dichotomous characteristics that define
one's dominant identity. It is the essential polarity in
order for one to be who one is, for without it, one cannot
be: the male, who is not female; the adult, who is not the
child; the human, who is not the beast; the living, who
is not the dead. As the opposite, it is the ultimate enemy,
the far point of the journey. It is not simply the enemy,
however, since it is one's other half. It is also the ultimate
beloved. As the other half of the self, it lurks forever
on the fringes of perception, yearning to reengage in an
agonistic embrace that is both battle and love.

This other person is a mythological theme worldwide. The Germans called it the *Doppelgänger* or 'double walker.' The Norse and the Finnish peoples thought
it walked in front of one as a view into the future. It is
commonly seen as a harbinger of misfortune and has
overtones of clairvoyant altered perception, a glimpse
of oneself caught in peripheral vision. It is probably
derived from the shamanic access to the experience of
bilocation, the ability to be simultaneously somewhere
else, or distant vision, seeing things somewhere else.

> Everyone carries a Shadow, and the less it is embodied in the individual's conscious life, the blacker and denser it is. If it is repressed and isolated from consciousness, it is liable to burst forth suddenly in a moment of unawareness.
>
> —C.G. Jung
> *Psychology and Religion*

The original state of spiritual confusion experienced by the seekers leads in modern therapy to an analysis and interpretation of irrational thoughts expressed in dreams and fantasies (anamnesis). The acceptance of this material from the unconscious widens the perspective and awareness of the conscious mind, and enables the enriched personality to better cope with its environment.

—C.G. Jung
The Personification of the Opposites

In psychotherapy, this unrecognized and rejected other may encroach upon the self and enact its hostility by manifesting itself as various psychoses. A cure is accomplished by a journey into the forgotten past, whose contents have been repressed into the subconscious. There one must confront oneself.

A battle ensues of heroic dimension. The outcome cannot be surrender by either side, since that would result in only half a person. The confrontation must end in reconciliation, so that the rejected self plays a proper recessive role in a bipolar stability expressing total integration. Such a person is an adult at peace with the child within, no longer subject to infantile fits of tantrum, or a male who can mediate with his own traits of femininity.

The Myth of the Hermaphrodite

An effective guide for this journey, which can be experienced either in psychoanalysis or in rites of initiation, is another of these strange creatures one encounters on a trip, the half-person or unilateral figure, a worldwide metaphor for the entheogen. It is also the face reflected in the mirror.

The Greek version of this unilateral creature is described in Plato's *Symposium*. The comedic playwright Aristophanes offers

Narratives featuring the half-man are found all over the globe.... It did not arrive at its vast distribution by way of diffusion... but it gives every indication of being a spontaneous expression of the imaginative unconscious.

—Rodney Needham
Circumstantial Deliveries

the myth of the half-person or one-sided creature as his contribution to the discussion of love at the drinking party. Originally, there were three sexes, male, female, and the hermaphrodite. These beings were total and perfect, spherical, with two faces in opposite directions, two sets of genitals, and eight limbs on which they could roll about with ease. The gods were jealous of their strength and spherical perfection, and they cut each in half to make them only half as strong. Then they turned each half's face and four remaining limbs inward, drawing the perimeter of the severed skin together with a drawstring like a purse at what is now called the *navel*. Forever after, they would have to see the scar left from their severance and seek to repair the separation by embracing their other half.

Hermaphroditic deity of creation

The poor creatures were doing this, but they were dying off, withering away, since their genitals were still on their backsides. The gods took pity on them and also moved the sex organs to the inner side. Thus the male could embrace his male counterpart, and the female her female other half. These were gay men and Lesbian women, but they might also under duress couple with the opposite sex and reproduce heterosexually, allowing the race of humans to continue in existence. The severed hermaphrodite, however, had a physical linkage with its other half in the corresponding sex organs of its opposite. Sex was really great for them. These half-hermaphrodites became creatures with an inordinate sexual drive: wanton women and profligate men, hypersexuality, as the psychologists label it, which is termed nymphomania in women and satyriasis in men.

Half-hermaphrodites became creatures with an inordinate sexual drive—wanton women and profligate men—hypersexuality which psychologists call nymphomania in women and satyriasis in men.

Dionysian theater

Plato put this speech in the mouth of the great comedian of the Dionysian theater. It is meant to be hilarious and outrageous. It is also, however, meant to encode something very true in the total context of the argument of the *Symposium*, which is the pathway to transcendent knowledge or revelation as the greatest of all loves. In Platonic philosophy, this is termed anamnesis, recognition and remembrance of one's former existence in the empyrean, one's truest other half.

The myth of the hermaphrodite is the tale of the origin of humankind, and it is a version of the Greek myth that humans were created out of mushrooms. The original spheres cut in half, with the skin drawn to the navel, radiating out with wrinkles, is a perfect likeness of the gill structures on the underside of the mushroom's cap, suitably anthropomorphized by the addition of a head, arms, and legs. If these new mushroom people did not behave themselves, the gods threatened to slice them in half again, leaving them with only a single leg on which to hop up and down, as mushroom one-foots.

Twin Sons of Zeus

A similar myth describes the twin sons of Zeus known as the *Dioscuri*, who were born from a single egg. They are so similar, although dissimilar, that one is mortal and the other immortal, but they have vowed to share each other's fate on alternating days. They, too, are anthropomorphized mushrooms, characterized by their mushroom caps and mushroom shields, which are the remnants of their split eggshell, and by a horizontal beam or pillar that connects the two.

The mushroom grows from an egg shape that separates into a lower and upper half by the thrust of the extending stipe, so that it comes to resemble a dumbbell. The navel of the radiating gills becomes the interconnection of the upper and lower halves, as the expanding cap, that at first appeared phallic, turns into the receptive vulva, and it appears now to copulate with itself as a hermaphrodite. This dumbbell plant was also known as the magical Promethean herb, a plant that grew with a double stem, half up, half down, to the hemispherical remnants of the split eggshell. No other plant can boast a double stem.

Rodney Needham draws attention to the wide dissemination of the 'Unilateral Figures' that are scattered around the world, from the Eskimos of the extreme North to the Yamaha of Tierra del Fuego, from the Nahua of Mexico to the folklore of Greece and Romania. If in the cultures where Needham finds 'unilateral figures' there was knowledge of the entheogens, here then will be proof that this ancient religion has existed even more widely than I thought.

—R. Gordon Wasson,
Persephone's Quest

The original role for drugs like LSD when it was offered to the market was its potential use in facilitating psychoanalytic analysis and in allaying the anxiety of patients suffering from a terminal illness. Classical mythology lay at the onset of the new science of psychoanalysis in the 19th Century since it seemed to encode some of the most basic paradigms of human existence as experienced in the Western world. However, because of the condemnatory reaction of professional Classicists to the Psychedelic Revolution, its rich compendium of significant tales was placed largely off limits for people trying to comprehend the meaning of their visionary experiences, and they were forced, as we have said, to seek out more exotic myths and religions.

This was unfortunate because not only are the Classical paradigms among the most perfected and best documented exemplars and, in addition, indigenous to the Western tradition, but they also evolved from ancient shamanic rites with psychoactive sacraments that were still practiced in the religions of the Classical and Hellenistic Greco-Roman periods, including Christianity. The Greek hero and heroine tales are potentially as significant to the psychic traveler as they were to the scientists who used them to map the human psyche. They also, as we shall see, are equally applicable for initiatory preparation for the terminal journey.

There is only one story, although the actors involved have many faces. In what follows, we will establish the themes that never change, the story that is the only story ever told, what Joseph Campbell termed the 'monomyth.' Its therapeutic value is there for anyone willing to confront the image reflected in the mirror or to journey like Alice into the rabbit hole. We add to it the central theme of the entheogen, which burst onto the scene after Campbell's formulation of the pattern. We also make more explicit what Freud and Jung, as scientists, were reluctant to confess publicly. What we reveal was also known to the great Sir George Frazer, author of *The Golden Bough* and Jane Ellen Harrison, of *Prolegomena to the Study of Greek Religion*, but except for tantalizing bits, students will seek in vain for them to mention openly anything so lowly as the fairies' mushroom.

There is only one story, although the actors involved have many faces.

Betwixt and Between

The best example of the paradigm from Classical mythology is the story of the hero Perseus. He was the first of the many heroes who followed and he performed only one essential task, and hence he is the easiest to understand. He harvested the Medusa's head. He picked the sacred mushroom. All the heroes that came after him, however, are variations upon the same mythic pattern. The shamanic motif of an entheogen is central to all these tales, but has gone largely ignored.

The shamanic motif of an entheogen is central to all these tales, but has gone largely ignored.

As with all the heroes, Perseus is 'liminal,' which is to say, he stands on the threshold or *limen* of a doorway that opens into different worlds on either side. In each he has an identity that mirrors the other, so that actually there are two heroes, one in either world, who would meet each other from opposite sides as they approach the doorway like a mirror. Since Classical Greek mythology evolved as reconciliation between an indigenous Anatolian-Mediterranean religious tradition where a goddess was supreme and an imported colonizing tradition occasioned by the immigration of a male dominant Nordic Indo-European culture with a supreme god, the hero has two possible roles to play. He can be either the subservient male of the former goddess or the male who dominates her in the service of the new presiding god.

It should be pointed out, however, that the cult of the mushroom was a shamanic tradition already established both among the Mesopotamian, Anatolian, Minoan Mediterranean, Egyptian, and Semitic peoples, and among the northern so-called Hyperborean immigrants. The ubiquity of the mushroom cults cannot be explained by physical contact between different cultures. It is most easily seen as the result of shamanic communion with the plant itself, reinforced by notions common to humanity, what Jung called the archetypes and Plato termed the remembrances and re-cognitions— *anamnesis*—from the empyrean.

The dual potential of the gateway is personified in the Roman god Janus, with a face in either direction. His epithet was 'two-face'—*bifrons*. Sometimes, like the hermaphrodite, his other face is female. He lends his name to the month of January, looking back at the year past and forward to the coming year. The janitor is named after him, not as the person who cleans the building, but as the one who controls passage through his doorway. The Egyptians had a similar deity who controlled the terminal passage across the marshlands that divide this world from the other. He was the boat-man named 'Face-in-front-face-behind.'

Key to Open Gateway

Standing on the threshold, betwixt and between, is the zoomorphic anthropomorphism of the key that opens the gateway. It is the actual reflected image of the entheogen. The reflection of the mushroom in the mirror of the doorway would be the olive tree. Reflected also is the dual potential for the hero who is consub-stantial with it and its deities. In one world, that of the goddess, there is the Medusa, queen of the sisterhood of Gorgons. In the other, that of the god, there is the subjugated goddess, Athena reborn as the daughter of the god, a female with no mother. She can forever testify that the male is the more important parent in procreation.

In fact, well into the Renaissance it was thought that the female contributed nothing to the develop-ing embryo but her body as an alchemical vessel. The invention of the microscope seemed at first to confirm this, since it made the spermatozoa —semen-animal-visible to the eye. The early scientists were thus enabled to see the 'little man' or *homunculus*, or the 'little ani-mal' or *animalcule* as proof of the male's total contribu-tion, an entire being already present in the male seed, even before it entered the womb.

Seeing Medusa and Athena

If Athena viewed her face in a mirror, she would see
the Medusa. The same would happen on the other side
as the Medusa looked upon her own reflected image.
In fact, the Medusa, as we have said, was not really a
terrifying monster. She was ravishingly beautiful, and
was so depicted sometimes even in ancient art. Cel-
lini's famous Florentine bronze statue of Perseus indicates that the tradition of her beauty persisted into the
Renaissance: the only thing monstrous in the depiction
is that the blood flowing from the decapitated head
is metamorphosing into coral, as an indication of her
fungal identity. Her beauty was the reason that she was
so dangerous to men, who would not be able to resist
her attractiveness or separate themselves from her after
intercourse. It was Athena who made her appear ugly.
On the other side of the mirrored image is Athena, a
beautiful female that no man would fantasize as a sexual
partner. She dressed as a man and was accepted as man's
best companion, attending him as a non-sexual girl
friend on his masculine pursuits.

As the hero stands on the threshold, he is consubstantial with the entheogen and with the goddess and
the god on either side. Here he is the half-creature,
with a foot in either world. Here he has a botanical
identity that partakes of the plant on either side. In
one world is the mushroom of the Gorgon head. In the
other is the olive tree of Athena. The creature in the
doorway is both male
and female, guardian
of the passage through,
either blocking the way
or affording access to
the shamanic flight.

It helps you open doors
to yourself. You can see
yourself for what you are.

—Ann Shulgin
Psychedelic Lay Therapist

This is the full ambiguity of the heroic persona. In psychedelic psychoanalysis, the psychoactive drug unlocks the door so that you pass through and 'see yourself for what you are.'

Surrogate Parents

Freud analyzed the complex dynamics of the nuclear family that resulted in the foundling fantasy. The child feels somehow out of place, unlike the siblings, alienated from the parents, probably somebody else's child: a found child or foundling, like Oedipus, picked up by a herdsman on the mountainside where he had been abandoned by his parents; or like Moses, abandoned in the basket floating down the Nile. In the lore of the fairies, such a child is a changeling, a child of the fairy folk left in exchange for the one they stole away. A fairy child would have a secret botanical identity, a consubstantial shamanic sacrament.

This ambiguity about the hero's parentage is essential to the mythical paradigm, often the reason why the hero passes through the doorway to find his other self. The hero on each side, in the reflected worlds, has a different set of parents.

Ritually, this was enacted in two ways. In androcentric theologies, a priestess could experience non-ordinary reproduction with a god. The human male through the

Androcentric Scenario: As [the Watchers] continued looking at the women, they were filled with desire for them and perpetrated the act in their minds. Then they were transformed into human males, and while the women were cohabiting with their husbands they appeared to them.

— *Testament of Reuben*

Gynocentric Scenario: From the muses one separated. She came to a high mountain and spent some time seated there, so that she desired her own body in order to become androgynous. She fulfilled her desire and became pregnant from her desire. He [the illuminator of knowledge] was born.

Revelation of Adam
—Marguerite Rigoglioso
The Cult of Divine Birth in Ancient Greece

agency of an entheogen became a surrogate for the god, possessed by the divine spirit as he inseminated the female. This is clearest in the myth of Hercules' mother, who slept with Zeus, who had assumed the appearance of her husband.

In gynocentric theologies, the priestess through the agency of an entheogen generated the spontaneous meiosis of her ovum, mimicking the ultimate parthenogenic capacity of the creator goddess in birthing the cosmos from the Void of her vulva, essentially cloning or replicating herself. This latter scenario, although beyond ordinary human experience, is apparently possible through the use of various toxins, probably derived from serpent venoms, to stimulate the division of the ovum. If this proved impossible, it was at least the mythologized history of the event. In both birthing scenarios, the entranced state is essential. The cloning might replicate the mother as her daughter, but it could also yield the birth of a divine son demonstrating the containment of the male within the female, a return to hermaphroditic unity.

In the mythic paradigm, the hero actually has *two fathers*, a mortal and a divine surrogate. The phrase is italicized here as the first of an enumeration of recurrent motifs that we will develop. The father of Perseus

was either his mother's uncle—Proëtus or Proïtos, or
the god Zeus. A maternal granduncle, which is the
relationship of Proëtus to Perseus, is seen as an intensi-
fication of female lineage. The surrogacy of the divine
father is always indicated by the chthonic or human
circumstances of the god's intervention, since in actual
fact the entranced human enacted the divine insemi-
nator. In the case of Perseus's mother, Danaë, she had
been buried beneath the earth, but Zeus inseminated
her via a shower of golden rain. Alternatively, the mortal and physical Proëtus may have found his way into
the subterranean confinement and became the father of
the hero.

In the Renaissance, Titian depicted the dual agency
as an alchemical theme. The heavens open above for
the rays of divine empyreal illumination to impreg-
nate Danaë. Beside her, the physical midwife catches
a shower of golden coins. The painting was so popular
that Titian made five versions for his noble patrons.

The mortal version of the *two fathers* motif, moreover, always has connotations of the gynocentric scenario. In addition to being the maternal granduncle,
Proëtus has a wife with an honorific name of female
dominance. She is called *Stheneboea* or 'Cow-strength.'
Apart from being the twin of Danaë's father and the pu-
tative father of Perseus, Proëtus is a figure of no impor-
tance. Stheneboea is the dominant force in their union.

There are also two mothers in the paradigmatic
hero tale, but the mother is more problematic. No one
can ever be sure about the father, but there were wit-
nesses for his physical emergence from his mother.
So the mother is a historical event, but what kind of
woman is she? There are always two different possibilities, which thematically indicate two different mothers.

She always has a background that would indicate that she was the dominant partner in the sexual relationship with her mate. The weakling mortal father and dominant female could have been the parental couple, producing a son beholden to his mother. This was the case with one version of Perseus. He repeatedly had difficulty separating himself from her. Thus, he was born in an underground chamber sequestered with her. Then, no sooner born than he was confined with her in a chest and set adrift on the sea. Ultimately, this sequestration with the mother derives from

Danaë being confined in a chest with her baby Perseus and Acrisius, Danaë's father

the gynocentric scenario. He really is just an extension of her hermaphroditic self-sufficiency.

Danaë came from a whole sisterhood of women who rejected sex with males. They were called the Danaïds as a group, and Danaë is one of them, three generations later. They so dominated their unloved and unnecessary partners that they slaughtered them in their bridal beds—all except for one. She turned against her own kind and was named Hypermnestra, a name that designates her as a female who accepts her role as a 'courted' woman, open for the androcentric scenario of matrimony.

9

Ⅾomoeroticism

The gynocentric scenario is mythically involved in connotations of Lesbianism, of women too close as a bound sisterhood to surrender their virginal condition. Virgin—*parthenos* in Greek—designates simply a female who has not accepted matrimony. They could have children, but they refuse to abandon the sisterhood. Their offspring were called bastards, which in Greek is the 'offspring of virgins.' The best exemplar of this is the troop of confirmed virgins who accompany the virgin goddess Artemis. One of them is Callisto. Zeus disguised himself as a female in order to engage her in sex.

Callisto was transformed into a bear and transported among the constellations as the Great Bear, Ursa Major—the Big Dipper. Her son, who was a bear, became the constellation Ursa Minor, the Little Bear. The visualization of the constellation as a bear can be traced back at least 13,000 years. This antiquity is obviously a result of oral mythical traditions since it requires a considerable amount of imagination to see the group of stars as a bear.

From Greek, 'virgin' designates a female who has not accepted matrimony because she refuses to abandon the sisterhood.

The seven stars of the constellation were seen as a pathway for the focus of spiritual energy from the empyrean back to the human race. The special prominence of the Great Bear constellation derives from the fact that two of its stars point to the north polar star (Polaris), which appears to be the immobile axis of the cosmos, around which the other constellations rotate. The pole star was imagined as the gateway through to the empyrean. In cultures that visualize the constellation differently, the mythic traditions indicate the same symbolic identification as a celestial psychoactive gateway. The Dipper, for example, derives from an African visualization that came to the Americas with the slave trade and implies a psychoactive potion that is drunk from the dipper. In Celtic lore, the constellation is the wheel of Arthur's Wain that will transport one to the empyrean. The pole star as the axle of a rotating wheel of metaphysical transport immediately suggests the gilled underside of a mushroom.

In contrast to the gynocentric sisterhoods, the various male mystical brotherhoods, such as the corybants and the Cabiri, are implicated in male homoeroticism and the birthing of non-physical Gnosis, the outcome of Platonic love. This persisted into the Zoroastrian religion assimilated into the Greco-Roman world as Mithraism, which in Greece was interchangeable with the cult of the hero Perseus. Mithraism admitted only male initiates and valued procreativity without the agency of female physicality.

The Danaïds who killed their husbands were condemned to death, and in the netherworld they forever
attempt to fill a basin with water for their prenuptial
bath, but it will never take place. Either they must
gather the water with sieves or the tub to contain it
leaks the water away. Perseus's mother could have taken
after these powerful, independent women, or she could
have been like the single ancestor who spared her
husband instead and accepted matrimony and the male
dominance of the androcentric scenario.

For this dual ambiguity about the mother's role, we
employ the label of turncoat. Danaë could have been a
turncoat to her own family heritage, which is italicized
as the second item in our enumeration of motifs, the
turncoat mother.

The hero thus has two
sets of parents, corresponding to the two scenarios. His
parents are either Zeus and
Danaë or Proëtus and Danaë,
with the mother having a
pivotal role of two possibilities, either the androcentric
turncoat—the female who
has changed sides in the battle to lend her support to
the androcentric scenario, or the woman true to her
unredeemed gynocentric heritage.

The hero has two
sets of parents—
either Zeus and Danaë
or Proëtus and Danaë,
with the mother hav-
ing a pivotal role of two
possibilities.

By Any Other Name

This produces two antithetical identities for the hero.
If there are two, do they have different names? Yes,
there are two, the motif of the *two names*—again italicized as the third in our enumeration of motifs. There is

Perseus and his double, a mysterious figure called Chrys-aor, who came into existence when Perseus successfully liberated him from confinement in his mother. Entrap-ment in the female is the gynocentric scenario.

When Perseus harvested the head of the Medusa, Chrysaor emerged triumphant from the severed neck, along with the magical flying horse Pegasus. He is named as the 'Golden Pluck,' consubstantial with the plucked head, which could also be metaphorically called the golden fruit cut from a sacred tree. Similarly, he is named as the pommel of the sword that Perseus meant to pluck when he plucked the mushroom at the site of Mycenae. The pommel of a sword was called its mushroom. The erect penis was also called a mush-room.

The *two names* motif also yields two ways of inter-preting the hero's name. Perseus has either a matrilineal name in the gynocentric scenario, derived from the mermaid Perse, who was the mother of the great witch Circe, who turned men into boars; and of the Cretan Pasiphaë, who lusted for the bull and who mothered the Minotaur; and of Aeëtes, who was the father of the witch Medea and the owner of the Golden Fleece. As a mermaid, Perse is essentially a doublet for the Gorgon Medusa.

The other possibility is that in overcoming the threat of the Medusa, he has mastered her power. In this case he has the ability to smite, strike, and ravage derived from the root that yields ferio in Latin. Thus, instead of being 'Perse's man,' he could be seen as the one with Perse's power to wield as a weapon to 'smite' his enemies.

Mushroom Man

There is still another possibility. He has an analogous identity as Bellerophon of Corinth. He is the only other hero to ride on the Medusa's son, the flying horse Pegasus. He is obviously a hero from an analogous way of telling the story. With this name, the hero is called the 'Slayer of Baal.' Baal—Ba'al—means 'Lord' and was the title of various deities in Anatolia, where the major part of Bellerophon's heroism takes place. Ultimately, Ba'al is merely the male attendant of the Lady Ba'alath in the gynocentric scenario, consort of the Canaanite goddess.

Pharaoh with emblems of shamanic empowerment, wearing the mushroom-shaped White Crown of Upper Egypt.

One of the names attested for that Canaanite goddess from a 7th Century BCE divinatory temple at Ekkron, just 35 kilometers southwest of Jerusalem, was Pitryh (pronounced pet-ree-yah), PTR, Hebrew for 'mushroom,' with the final syllable a suffix indicating divinity, as in the name of Yahweh. The patriarchal revisionism that resulted in the canonic Old Testament understandably considered Ba'al a false god. Ba'al was called Ba'al Zebub, 'Lord of the Flies,' an attribute hard to disassociate from the folkloric traditions of the fly-agaric mushroom, the *Amanita muscaria*. Christian demonology identified him with the fallen angel

of the illumination, Lucifer. He was thought to materialize as a toad, enthroned upon his toadstool. Christian
hagiography turned PTR into Peter, the crucified saint
and first of the popes, the 'rock'—Greek petros—upon
which the Vatican stands.

A bronze figurine of Ba'al from the 14th-12th Century BCE found at ancient Ugarit depicts him with an
elongated mushroom cap, in the style of the White
Crown or hedjet of Upper Egypt—southern Egypt,
upstream of the Nile—worn by the pharaohs. It is elongated, tapering to a knob on top, producing the characteristic shape of a bowling pin. The mushroom shape
of these crowns is so obvious that Joussef Abubakr,
who wrote the definitive study of the Egyptian crowns,
described the Pharaoh Sesostris' version as "pilzartige
Form" or mushroom-shape.

He did not realize, of course, just how appropriate
his characterization of this crown was or the reason for
the crown's enigmatic shape. It strongly suggests that
the pre-dynastic ancestors of the Egyptian pharaohs
were shamanic herbalists who came to believe that
they were divine and immortal through pharmaceutical
rituals. Shamans traditionally dress with the emblems of
their empowerment.

Thus Bellerophon, like his doublet Perseus, is also
consubstantial with a mushroom, and associated with
a goddess in a cult of the mushroom. His name as the
'Slayer of Ba'al,' indicates that Bellerophon's other
name would have been Ba'al. In the same way, Hermes,
as the Olympian androcentric deity, had an earlier
identity in the gynocentric scenario as Argos. Thus he
could be called the 'Slayer of Argos' or Argeïphontes.
Perseus gave one of his daughters a similar name as
Gorgophonë.

These are the recurrent motifs of the monomyth: two fathers, a turncoat mother, and two names. We now add a fourth, the motif of botanic consubstantiality. Bellerophon and Perseus both have characteristics that suggest a fungal anthropomorphism that they share with their Ladies, the 'Queen' Medusa and the Lady Ba'alath.

Transcendence or Decadence

There were, moreover, two possible outcomes from Perseus's encounter with the Medusa in her cave confinement. She could have turned him into a phallic pillar of stone, so that he never separated from her. Such phallic stones or priapic pillars may have been employed in the gynocentric scenario to stimulate the virginal orgasm considered necessary to initiate the meiosis of the ovum. Perseus would have merged totally with her as her masculine entity, like Shiva—*lingam*—and Parvati—*yoni*—in the Cave of the hermaphrodite. This is a symbolic pattern that can be traced back to the Paleolithic mushroom pillars or dolmens and the sacred caves of initiation.

The other outcome was that Perseus liberated himself as Chrysaor from the confinement of her body, the successful plucking of the mushroom's head. In the Paleolithic scenario, traversing the permeable magic of the rock paintings to escape into the empyrean enacted such an outcome. In this version of the Perseus myth, the magical horse, the steed called Pegasus and named for the spring with its entheogenic waters, emerged along with Chrysaor from the severed stipe or neck. The horse represents acquiring the shamanic empowerment conferred by the entheogen.

Merely for convenience in labeling the two possibilities, the former could be called 'descendent' and the latter 'ascendant,' as directions along the cosmic axis through the volcanic mountain from the alchemical crucible to the fiery empyrean. These labels imply no value judgment. They simply reflect the prejudice of the chauvinism implicit in the evolution of the Classical male-dominant tradition.

The flying winged horse is the vehicle for his shamanic transport. On its back, with the golden pluck securely stored in his herbalist sack—which is what a kibisos is, a kind of lunch bag that Hermes lent him—he escapes from the cave and from the pursuit of the Medusa's Gorgon sisters. Among the Medusa's zoomorphic attributes was her horse characteristic, and both Chrysaor and the flying horse Pegasus are her children. Liberated now from confinement in the mother and with the head of the Medusa as his empowerment, Perseus flies through the doorway to his identity as the male who is dominant over the female in the androcentric scenario.

Thus he spies the maiden Andromeda chained to a pillar of stone. As her name indicates, she is a double of the Medusa and of himself as the pillar imprisoned in her cavern-womb-vulva. Andromeda means 'Male' (andro-) 'Ruler' (meda-, medousa). With the power of the harvested head of the mushroom entheogen, he liberates the maiden as his wife and flies off to turn all the marriage guests at the wedding feast for Hippodamia into pillars of stone. The bride is named as the 'horse-dominant-female.' There are various tales about her, but in all the myths, she is merely an epithet of the

> The flying winged horse is the vehicle for shamanic transport.

Medusa. Freud recognized that the Medusa represented the emasculation of the male.

In displaying the Gorgon head at the wedding feast, Perseus has enacted the complete reversal of what he would have been if he had never separated himself from his mother, or if he had never soared from the Cave. This is the tale of the transcendent or ascendant version of his dual identity. It is the story of Perseus, whose name means the 'one who smites,' and of Chrysaor, the hero whose heroic power resides in his successful harvest of the golden pluck.

Since there are two personae, however, or two names with a different set of parents, there is another way of telling the tale, with a completely opposite outcome. This is the decadent or descendent version.

Perhaps Perseus wasn't the child of Zeus and the turncoat mother. Suppose Danaë hadn't succumbed to the androcentric pattern of divine birthing, and Proëtus was his actual father—Proëtus, who is the weakling male dominated by his Lady, the 'strong cow.' The decadent potential of Proëtus as the hero's father had begun even two generations earlier, since as Danaë's uncle, he was the twin brother of her father Acrisius. The two brothers had begun fighting each other while they were still in their mother's womb.

This is how the tale is told in its decadent version. Perseus showed up at the citadel of Proëtus, and in a dispute over entheogens, his half-sisters, the daughters of his stepmother Stheneboea, metamorphosed into a Gorgon sisterhood, mooing like cows in estrus. They turned into mushrooms, with scabby red skin, and plucked

> The terror of the Medusa is thus a terror of castration.
> —Sigmund Freud
> *The Medusa's Head*

him, tearing him limb from limb. Instead of empower-
ing him, the entheogen and its metaphoric mythic
complex overpowered him.

Enemy as Friend

The recurrent motifs enumerated thus far are the two
fathers; two types of mother, with one perhaps a turncoat to her own dominant lineage; two names; and botanic consubstantiality. Since there are two versions of
the liminal hero in the doorway, there are two scenarios
for his career enacted, one in each world on either side
of the threshold, the transcendent—ascendant—and
the decadent—descendant.

The motif of the *two names* can also be enacted in
the birthing of dissimilar twins or warring brothers or
sisters. Such was the case with the Dioscuri, and also
their twin sisters, Helen and Clytemnestra. In the myth
of Hercules, he was born as the son of Zeus, while his
twin brother Iphicles was born from the seed of the
mortal Amphitryon, with their mother playing a dual
role as turncoat or not, in the androcentric and gynocentric scenarios.

There are two more motifs to complete the reper-
tory of themes. These are the figures that help the hero,
the enablers, in the transcendent tale, or the figures
who disable him in the decadent version.

Enablers help the hero in the transcendent tale and figures dis-able him in the
descendant. Perseus had allies to guide his
trip. Typically, there are two, the motif of the helpers, one male and one
female, the inspiring winds for the
journey of the soul, an animus and
anima. The metaphor of the wind
indicates the role of the entheogen,

since 'inspire' means 'take or put in wind.' Both Latin words signify essentially a 'wind,' but one is grammatically masculine, and the other feminine. Thus they conveniently can name the male helper or friend and the female helper.

An anima leads a woman into a deeper understanding of her femaleness. An animus leads a male to confront the darker aspects of his masculinity.

Anima & Animus

We are proposing a somewhat broader interpretation than Jung's use of these terms, since he assigns an anima to a male and an animus to a female. Both males and females have both a male and female guide, inasmuch as all humans are basically hermaphroditic, with one sexual identity dominant over the other, but still present. An anima would lead a woman into a deeper understanding of her femaleness; it is limiting to assume that a woman needs only to access her masculine nature, and a male his female. An animus would lead a male to confront the darker aspects of his masculinity.

The negative potential of the Medusa is her power to inanimate, to suck the wind out and make one into the inanimate pillar locked in her cave. These helpers, the animus and anima, are the male and female aspects of the very monster blocking the doorway or lurking in the worlds beyond, transmuted and pacified—if they act as helpers. Rejected, they revert to enemies and play the role of disablers in myth. In the same way, the entheogen can be either mastered or mastering and overpowering.

In many of the hero tales, the female helper is the pacified Medusa, the mirror image of her dominant power. This pacified transmutation is the goddess Athena, who wears the plucked Gorgon head as a commemoration of her former self.

Hermes, whose iconography and myth indicate his former identity as a phallic pillar, plays the role of male guide. He could be represented merely as a male pillar, and even when completely anthropomorphized, he often is represented attached to a pillar. This pillar is an essential item in his iconography and is not needed as a support to allow the statue to stand upright. Both the anima and the animus are the enemy who has been transmuted into a guide or enabler for the heroic event.

It is a reciprocal dependency, however, since Athena needs the hero to pluck the Medusa's head, in order for her to be Athena, instead of the Gorgon. The same is true of Hermes. It was he who lent the hero the flying sandals for his journey to the doorway and the herbalist sack in which to deposit the plucked head.

Hermes, with pillar support, School of Praxiteles, known as 'Antinous Belvedere.'

Freud was aware that he was acting as a soul guide for his patients into the repressed and darker aspects of their personae. In the course of evolving his therapeutic procedure of psychoanalysis, he gathered a collection of little figurines of ancient deities on his desk, using them as his guides. His favorite was a bronze of Athena, which he often fingered in the course of the consultation. It was perfect, he said, except that it had something missing. A missing part is never really missing, it is somewhere else, a perfect symbol for the journey of the unilateral figure across the threshold to find its missing other half.

The hero's conquest of the numinous power dwelling within the entheogen creates the particular iconographic persona of the deity. The consubstantiality of the trio, the human, the plant, and the deity, is the compact man makes with the divine. This is a compact that must be continually reenacted through ritual and the prescribed herbal procedures for addressing the entheogen.

Otherwise, the compact is undone, and Athena reverts to the Medusa and hinders, instead of helping. She did this, for example, to the hero Ajax, who expressly stated that he would accomplish his hero-ism on his own without any help from her. Instead of being empowered by the ecstasy that he 'harvested,' he plucked the madness, in which state he thought he was being a hero, but he saw only the delusion of his heroism and did the op-posite of his potential dual identity. The metaphor of 'harvesting the madness' is the way that the tragedian Sophocles described the event.

Freud, who pioneered the journey of the soul, had a pantheon of little deities on his desk. His favorite was a bronze statuette of Athena, which he would often hold as a guide in his psychoanalytic sessions. He particu-larly loved it since it was broken, the missing part providing a link to another world where it must still survive. During his analysis of H.D., he picked it up and handed it to her. 'This is my favorite,' he said. 'She is perfect . . . only she has lost her spear.'

—Hilda Doolittle
Tribute to Freud

The Shadow

A version of the helper animus of the dichotomous hero on the shamanic quest is the motif of the shadow friend or companion. This brings us back to where we began with the theme of the Doppelgänger. It is responsible for some of the most profound works of literature. The best-known occurrence is the pairing of Achilles and Patroclus—Patrocles—at the Trojan War. The basic theme of the *Iliad* is the proxy death of Achilles in the persona of his beloved cousin, which temporarily satisfies the fated identity of Achilles as a hero born to fail. The death of Patrocles frees him to have his moment of glory in a battle that is finally put to an end by the gods since Achilles' potential victory threatens the stability of the world over which the gods preside. As an oral poem, the *Iliad* is the product of centuries or even millennia of evolutionary modification, making it an expression of perfected motifs of shamanic and psychological origin.

> The Greek hero Ajax has rejected Athena's help and in retaliation she has driven him mad. In his deluded vision, when he first sees her, he says: Oh Athena, hail, thou full of grace. How right it is that I see you now!
>
> —Sophocles
> *Ajax*

The Sumerian cuneiform epic of *Gilgamesh* preserves the same motif of the shadow companion in the figure of the king's friend, the wild-man Enkidu, whose death triggers the journey of Gilgamesh to the underworld to learn the secret of eternal life. Since the poem was recorded from various sources and was not the product of a single performance, as was the case of the

Iliad, it has themes extraneous to the purified shamanic nucleus, but it is not difficult to recognize the anthropomorphized equivalent of the Gorgon Medusa's fungal identity in the episode of Humbaba, the guardian of the Cedar Mountain, where the gods lived. The civilizing king and the friend from the wilds form an obvious antithetical dichotomy. The king needs his beloved friend from the woods in order to confront the monster in the wilderness.

Humbaba is often depicted as just a head with staring eyes and flowing beard and wild hair. Like the Medusa, his head was harvested and placed in a sack. Gilgamesh, the king of Uruk, and his wild-man companion Enkidu, the primordial Adam, formed from clay—there could not be a better portrayal of the hero and his animus mediator with the monstrous fungal Humbaba, guardian of the cedar forest that is home of the gods that fruit as the mushrooms symbiotic on the roots of the cedars of the Lebanese mountains

Humbaba is often depicted as just a head with staring eyes and flowing beard and wild hair.

Humbaba is probably the Anatolian goddess Cybele or Kubaba, her male consort or hermaphroditic persona, like the Greek Hermes. The depictions of Humbaba as the decapitated head show a face emerging from a labyrinthine complex representing the entrails of the sacrificial bull/cow as the digestive pathway to transcendence, often analogous to the womb markings on the belly of the goddess.

In Greek mythology, the same motif of the hero and mediator companion is represented as Hercules and his nephew Iolaüs—Iolaös. The nephew accompanies the hero on many of his heroic tasks, all of which

are metaphoric for encountering the goddess and her
zoomorphic toxins. The antithetical version of Hercules
was born as his twin Iphicles: Hercules from the seed
of Zeus, and Iphicles from the seed of the mortal father
Amphitryon. Iphicles' son Iolaüs, the nephew of Hercules, represents a pacified mediation with the opposite
twin.

The shadow companion can be added to the enumeration of recurrent motifs. It is a special type of animus or anima, differing in that the helper is not a deity,
but a human. The same motif can be seen in the paring
of the hero Theseus with his friend Pirithoüs. Pirithoüs
comes from the tribe of Lapiths of Thessaly and is usually depicted as a horseman. The two collaborated in
battling the drunken centaurs at Pirithoüs's wedding to
Hippodamia. The 'horse-dominant' name of the bride
is the same as in the Perseus story, and the horseman
companion helping to battle the centaur horsemen
indicates again that the shadow companion is playing
the same role as in the animus motif.

Our Lady of the Sea

The Medusa mythic configuration was too powerful to
die with the conversion of the Greco-Roman world to
Christianity and the purported demise of paganism. It
stretched back to the Paleolithic dawn of consciousness
and resurfaced in the medieval period where she was
assimilated as an aspect of the Virgin Mary. The hero
Hercules confronted her way back in mythical history
as the nymph of Scythia, and his Scythian descendants
commemorated her mushroom consubstantiality by
wearing golden fungal caps as ornaments on their belts
in battle.

As we have seen, in addition to being a sow, cow, serpent, bird, and horse, the Medusa was also a fish. She was a mermaid. Among the zoomorphic transmutations of the mushroom is the fish, so that the spore-bearing structures beneath the little creature's cap are called gills. She comes by this naturally in being a terrestrial version of the aquatic sponge. Medusa is a common name in Greek for the jellyfish. Jerome misinterpreted the etymology of Mary's name in Hebrew and endowed her with the epithet of Star of the Sea, *Maris Stella*. In doing this, the great scholar, who translated the bible into Latin, was probably misled by the mythical configuration of the ancient goddess and her association with springs and the waters of the sea.

In this aquatic manifestation, she surfaced from rivers and springs throughout medieval Europe as Melusina, the Mother of Light, a fairytale mushroom who empowered the dynasties of the ruling elite, including both the Valois of France and the Plantagenets of Burgundy and England. She granted infinite wealth and dominion to her chosen knight, on the one condition that he not see her on one special day of the week, when she bathed, revealing that her lower half was a serpent or a fish.

10

A Stunning Beauty

The heroine paradigm differs from that of the male hero. There are three faces reflected in the mirror. The two versions of the female's pathway to heroism are seen in the contrasting myths of Hecuba, the Queen of Troy, and the tale of Eros and Psyche.

The paradigm for the dual versions of the male hero's career corresponds to the physiological changes that are occasioned by the onset of puberty. The duality of the male paradigm, however, does not correspond to the physiology of a female's development. In addition to puberty, the female experiences a second change occasioned by menopause. There are three stages to a female's experience.

In addition, males and females seem to have a different instinctual way of reacting to the other members of their sex. Men typically mark out a territory and defend it against other male intruders. They relate to other men antagonistically, either in sport individually or as a team, against another team or an opposing army. Sport is a pacified version of war. In myth, the male confronts himself beyond the reflected image in the mirror.

Females, however, tend to group together. This bonding, moreover, in societies or situations where women live sequestered together, affects their reproductive cycles, so that they tend to synchronize their menstruation, not only with each other, but also with the phases of the moon. Its three periods (waxing, full, and waning) contrast with the diurnal and annual solar phases that are associated with the male. Both sun and moon experience a disappearance and return (night, new moon).

There is still another major difference between the sexes in their experience of living. Puberty for the male liberates him from the family and sends him out to confront the challenge of his identity. For the female, however, both the onset of menstruation at puberty and its cessation at menopause are more troubling changes, with disturbing emotional symptoms leading them into the mysteries of their own bodies. Pregnancy and motherhood, in addition, tie the female down to a particular place.

The old woman, who has lived through both physiological transitions, becomes the bearer of secret knowledge, not only about females, but also about their synchronicity with the cycles of nature and the cosmos and their closer association with Gaia or the Earth. Typically, this also involves expertise with medicinal and magical plants. Since these women were once the gateway into life through birthing, they also control the passage into death through the rituals of burial.

Michelangelo's sculpture of the Pietà ('Our Lady of Sorrows') depicted the Virgin mother and the crucified Son as a female and a male of the same age, and the gestures of their fingers employed the conventional symbolism of the Renaissance to indicate that they

Pietà, known as Our Lady of Sorrows

were lovers. The Pietà is erotic. The Virgin shows no signs of grief, but radiates majestic serenity. This makes the birthing mother into the gateway into death. Similarly, in the depictions of the death of the Virgin, termed the Dormition—Falling Asleep—or the Ascension, it was a commonplace to depict the Christ Child as an infant at the old woman's deathbed. After the Ascension, Mary was elevated to the Queen of Heaven—Regina Coeli, the spouse of her own resurrected son Jesus.

The Way of the Goddess

There are paradoxically three faces, three halves, reflected in the mirror for the female: the maiden, the mother, and the crone. Each face poses a riddle of identity for a woman. This enigma constitutes the female's heroic quest. These three stages of the female and their paradox are expressed in the figure of the goddess Hecate. She is always depicted as a triad of three women, back to back, carrying various ritual mystery implements and sometimes with differing headgear, but always all three are identical maidens, although Hecate was in her totality the reunion of maiden, mother, and crone. Together, they are the patrons of the secrets of witchcraft and the power of the female.

Hecate

Hecate is the guardian of the juncture where one road branches into two other directions. As such, the three roads of Hecate are a perfect comparison to the two masculine roads of Janus, who sometimes, as we mentioned, can have a female face, as well as a male, as suggestive of the male's femininity. In addition, Hecate symbolizes the role of the midwife and the wet nurse, the mysteries of birthing and breastfeeding. The wet nurse was usually a woman who had lost a child and by prolonging lactation nursed another woman's living child as replacement with the milk intended for her own child now resident in the otherworld. Hecate, therefore, has close affiliation with the lower world, and typically, one of the destinations offered where three roads meet is down. A dog, with its connotations of the wolf, was sacrificed to her at the crossroads. It was an animal that wasn't eaten, but simply left to rot.

> Hecate expresses the three states of the female and her riddle of identity.

In Greek mythology, Hecate presided over the reunion of the goddess Demeter (Roman Ceres) and her daughter Persephone. Hades had abducted the daughter into the netherworld. Hecate accompanied Persephone on her cyclical return to her mother as a visitor to the empyrean.

Typically, women reunited as a holy sisterhood for ritual enactments, grouping themselves generically as maidens, mothers, and crones. Such a triple bonding characterized the plant-gathering rituals of the bacchants. The male spiritual attendant in the service of the goddess was usually triple to match the trinity of the goddess. In Christianity, this motif is represented in

the three persons of the godhead and their relationship
to the Blessed Virgin and to the female Church who is
the Lord's spouse.

These triple sisterhoods abound in Classical myth.
The three fates were sometimes portrayed as a version
of Hecate. In the Perseus myth, three Grey Ladies, the
Graeae, guarded the final entrance into the Gorgon
Medusa's cave. The visionary or shamanic motif of the
passage into the cave was indicated by the single disembodied eye that they all three shared. Perseus passed
through invisible, as the eye was in transit among them.

A similar trinity was the triple sisterhood of Grac-
es, who attended the goddess Aphrodite, whom the
Romans called *Venus*, the goddess of love. Antonio
Canova depicted them as three females so amorously
involved with each other's beauty that they seem to
deny access to a man.

The Myth of Hecuba

The best narrative of the female's access to this awesome power of the triple goddess is Euripides' *Hecuba*
tragedy. Hecuba is named *Hekabe* in Greek. Hecuba was
recognized in antiquity as Bendis, a Thracian version of
Hecate. Hecate was called *Hekate* in Greek. It is often
said that the heroines in Greek mythology are versions
of a goddess.

Hekate—Hecate—and Hekabe—Hecuba—are
the same name. Bendis was worshipped in the phases
of the moon as a version of Artemis and presided over
the virginal sisterhood of the hunt. Although a virgin,
Artemis was also a midwife and a wet nurse, and she
was invoked as an aid for the psychological and physiological distress of menstruation.

The mythologized history of Troy made Hecuba into the queen of the city, the wife of King Priam. She supposedly bore him fifty children. The joy of motherhood is multiplied in the plurality of the offspring. The more children lost, however, the greater is the grief. The joyous mother becomes the Lady of Sorrows.

After the fall of Troy, the old queen was rounded up with the other women of Troy to be shipped off to Greece as captive slaves. Hecuba has already lost most of her children in the destruction of her city, but she still has two daughters and two sons remaining. Two of these surviving children are twins, both of them prophets or shamans, Cassandra and her brother Helenus. Hecuba had sent the other son, Polydorus, to a supposed ally to keep him safe. The daughters can expect only to be used as concubines of their victorious Greek masters. The same fate awaits the other captive women. Those too old for sex will perform other menial tasks. Helenus, who is the only one who will eventually survive, had actually turned against the Trojans and revealed the magical secrets about how the city could be destroyed.

The play begins with the ghost of Polydorus narrating that his supposed host Polymestor has murdered him to steal his secret horde of Trojan gold and that the Greeks intend to sacrifice his sister Polyxena as an offering to the tomb of Achilles in order to rouse a wind for the return home. Meanwhile Hecuba, offstage inside her tent, is having a nightmare that is a symbolic version of the same revelation about her daughter's sacrifice. She comes out of the tent crawling in terror. As the action proceeds, she begs

Hecuba was rounded up with the other women of Troy to be shipped off to Greece as captive slaves.

Hecuba is no longer a mother, but a crone, and she falls to the ground, groveling in the dust. Odysseus to intervene, since she once saved his life when he was found inside the city. He argues legalistically that he does indeed owe her a favor, but not her daughter. Hecuba curses such legalese and begs her daughter to supplicate Odysseus directly, but he pulls aside, and Polyxena disdains to beg for her life.

This gesture of supplication is a formal ritual that would bind the person petitioned to grant the petitioner's supplication. The petitioner abjectly embraced the other person around the knees and reached an arm up to touch the chin. Hecuba pleads to be sacrificed instead, or even with her daughter, but Odysseus bluntly says that the tomb doesn't want an old woman. She is no longer a mother, but a crone, and she falls to the ground, groveling in the dust.

After the sacrifice, the corpse of Polyxena is brought on stage, and the captive women, who have gone to the shore for water to wash the body to prepare it for burial, return with the corpse of the murdered son, which had washed ashore. With two dead children now visually present on stage, Hecuba plots revenge. She is the crone who mothered dead children.

She needs time before the Greeks set sail. The same actor who had played Odysseus now enters as Agamemnon. The doubling of roles is thematically significant. It is an indication of what the playwright intended as the structural meaning of the play. It was also something noted by the audience since a prize was awarded for the best actor, which means that the audience followed the actor through the succession of roles he impersonated. Odysseus had repulsed the gesture of ritual supplication, which would have bound him to return a favor, but now as Agamemnon the same actor begs Hecuba to ask what favor she seems to want. She just wants time before they set sail, but she tells him that if he helps her, her daughter Cassandra will be grateful and return the favor by greater sexual compliance in his bed as his concubine. This is extraordinarily amoral for the mother to use her daughter's rape as a ploy for her own empowerment. She is essentially acting as a pimp for her own daughter.

The revenge is enacted in the same tent where Hecuba had her nightmare at the play's beginning, but this time it is she who orchestrates the terrifying vision. Again, the structural balance is an indication of the playwright's intention. The tent is the Cave of Dreams, or more explicitly, nightmares.

The same actor in succession impersonates the roles of Polydorus—the son, Polyxena—the daughter, and Polymestor—the host who perverted hospitality by murdering his guest. It takes little imagination to notice that the three names are very similar. Polydorus is named for the 'great gift' of the horde of gold that his host has stolen. Polyxena is named as the 'great hostess' who was given as a gift to the tomb of Achilles. The sacrifice upon Achilles' tomb was a ritual of sexual abduction into the hospitality of the netherworld. Polymestor is named as the 'great advisor.' He is Hecuba's son-in-law, the man who ritually abducted her daughter in the ceremony of matrimony. Hecuba is his mother-in-law, to whom she gave her oldest daughter as a bride.

Polymestor was supposed to have been the host
for Hecuba's now dead son. She now offers him similar hospitality. She invites him and his two sons—her
grandsons—into the tent, enticing him with the prom-
ise of still more Trojan gold buried inside, the stolen
gift of Polydorus. The tent is filled with captive women,
women who have lost their children or are about to
serve as unwilling sexual slaves. The nubile ones, the
maidens, paw over Polymestor's robes, admiring the
fine texture of his wife's weaving—Hecuba's daughter,
until he realizes that his robes have trapped him like a
spider's web. Meanwhile the women who were mothers
have been cooing over the adorable two sons, handing
them from one to another to move them to the other
side of the tent until, with their father now captive in
his wife's web, the mothers murder the sons as the last
thing that the father would ever see. The maidens then
plunge their brooches into his eyes.

Female Role Conversion

These females have inverted their generic roles of sexually abducted maidens and birthing mothers, inflicting
their own pathetic roles upon their male enemy. The
maidens rape the rapist. The mothers kill the rapist's
sons. Hecuba, who is too old for sex, assists in the rape
of her prophetic daughter, who will be murdered by
Agamemnon's wife when they get back home.

Hecuba dances out of the tent in triumph, while
this time it is Polymestor who crawls out to tell his
nightmare. The two contrasting emergences from the
tent are choreographic parallels, the structure intended
by the playwright.

Hecuba is now in control, no longer the despised
old woman, but revealed in all her terrible power. She,

who had condemned the legalistic argument of Odysseus, now delivers a full legal justification for her revenge. Polymestor can retaliate only by foretelling Hecuba's fate. She will never reach Greece, but will fall from the mast of the ship at a place called 'dog's tomb,' plunging down into the netherworld to become a bitch among the goddesses known as the Furies.

Orestes Pursued by the Furies
by John Singer Sargent

We might well ask what she was doing climbing the mast of the ship. The ship's mast is metaphoric for the axis between realms. These Furies hound with madness whoever perverts the rights of motherhood. The last view Polymestor had before he lost his eyesight was of the females, united as a sisterhood and laying claim to their usurped matriarchal powers. It is this terrifying or stunning vision that has made him clairvoyant.

Something New

The ecstatic reversal of the creator of the universe to its destroyer is represented in the Hindu pantheon as the great goddess Kali. Hecuba, however, presents a more structured multi-dimensional configuration, since Kali simply whirls in one direction for a period of ages and then reverses direction to undo what she created.

Hecuba is the paradigm of the heroine who traverses the image reflected in the doorway to access the power of her totality as a female, approaching Hecate's

Thetis begs a favor of Zeus in gesture of supplication by Jean-Auguste-Dominique Ingres

crossroad from three directions, or passing through the reflection onto the branching roads to join her other two groups of sisters. Medea and Clytem-nestra similarly access this awesome power, knowingly and with full intention. These are the decadent versions of the heroine's story, although the term would be bet-ter phrased descendent, since there is nothing morally decadent about such triumphs.

In general, the other great heroines of the tragic stage try to deflect their potential for this power, but stumble upon it inadvertently. Both wives of Hercules, for example, have such experiences. Dejanira—Deiani-ra—in Sophocles' *Women of Trachis* cannot believe the tales of the great queen Omphalë who was so dominant that she and the hero exchanged roles and clothing. Yet she sends the returning hero her robe anointed with a love potion, without realizing that the toxin came from the centaur that he killed on their nuptial journey and that a love potion binds the lover to the other's will.

Hercules' other wife, Megara of Thebes, in Eurip-ides' *Herakles* is unaware that she is named as the 'Tomb Chamber' and she inadvertently sets in motion the recycling of the heroic toxins that will end in Heracles' placement in his tomb. The actor who had played Meg-ara, in fact, comes back in the role of Theseus to make arrangements for the burial. Between those two roles, the same actor impersonates the goddess of the wolf-madness called rabies, recycling back to Hercules the toxins that he had mastered in his ascendant version of heroism.

The Myth of Eros and Psyche

In these descendent versions of the heroine, she returns to the bonding with the triple sisterhood and its awesome power. There is also another way of telling the story. In this other version, the female is separated from her sisters and achieves ascendancy to the empyrean by reintegration with her devastatingly stunning beauty.

This is the tale of Eros and Psyche. Eros is the god of Love, the son of Aphrodite. Psyche means the 'Breath of Soul.' The tale is extant in the Latin novel of *The Golden Ass by* Apuleius , but it had Greek antecedents, now lost. The Latin version calls Aphrodite, Venus, and her son, Cupid. As an episode in a novel, it has undergone elaborations, like the multiple sources of *Gilgamesh*, which obscure some aspects of the archetypal pattern. Psyche and Eros, however, were already a tale, with religious implications, a full half millennium before they surfaced in *The Golden Ass*. As early as the late archaic period Psyche was depicted with butterfly wings, and that portrayal became a commonplace in Hellenistic art.

Psyche as Nature's Mirror
by Paul Thurman.

Psyche means both "inspiring breath of soul" and "butterfly," the inverse of the stunning beauty lurking behind the Gorgon Medusa.

In addition to meaning the 'inspiring breath of soul,' psyche is also the common word in ancient Greek for 'butterfly.' As the inspiring breath that animates life, psyche is obviously the inverse version of the stunning beauty that lurks beneath the monstrous iconography that portrays the Gorgon Medusa with her power to render the male inanimate and inseparable from her as her stone phallic pillar.

Psyche Butterfly

The psyche butterfly is emblematic of the metamorphosis of the voraciously eating caterpillar, creeping upon the plants that are its food, into the beautiful flying creature that no longer even has a mouth, and whose sole organ is reproductive. For the transformation, the caterpillar enters the chrysalis stage, secreting an exoskeleton as its cocoon. The creature inside is a pupa or little person, a 'doll,' and called the chrysalis because of its 'golden' color. When it emerges from the cocoon, an action called eclosion, the little doll bursts from the shell of its private cave enclosure, transformed into the beautiful butterfly. Both the botanical diet of the caterpillar and the pupa doll suggest the motif of visionary experience, since the pupil of the eye is so named as the little 'doll' seen reflected in its tiny mirror. The reflection, of course, is the minuscule image of the person outside gazing in through the watery membrane as the gateway to the other's soul.

The butterfly's sole function is the sexual union with another. Butterflies, however, are not promiscuous.

They are monogamous. The male caps the reproductive system of its mate, sealing it with a sphragis or vaginal plug after insemination. It also secretes a pheromone

The butterfly's sole function is the sexual union with another.

that repels other suitors. This scenario was observed in antiquity and Aristotle described it.

Psyche was so beautiful that people were beginning to call her another Aphrodite. The goddess grew jealous and commanded her son Eros to prick her with his poisoned arrow so that when she awoke from her sleep she would fall in love with whatever creature she first saw. Aphrodite intended this to be some hideous beast like the goat-man Pan. Shakespeare used this motif in his *Midsummer Night's Dream*, where the fairy queen Titania falls hopelessly in love with the ass-headed Bottom because of a magical herb. Both the ass and bottom imply the same obscenity.

Psyche, however, awoke unexpectedly and startled Eros. She looked right through him, but he was invisible. He pricked himself instead, falling madly in love with her. Aphrodite then put a curse on Psyche so that no one would ever want her. Disconsolate, Eros refused to continue his mission of spreading love around the world. Psyche was his one and only love.

Although Psyche is still beautiful, no one would take her for a wife. There was some kind of uncanny smell about her. An oracle informed her parents that they must abandon her on the nearby mountain. The wind abducted her to a paradisiacal valley with a magnificent palace, where invisible servants attended her. When night came, Eros consummated the marriage in the darkness, but he told her that she must never light a lamp to look upon him. They continued for some time in this manner of invisible love.

Psyche became pregnant and was allowed to visit
her two sisters. They were jealous of her bliss and con-
vinced her that her lover was some monstrous serpent
that would devour her and the child. That was the reason that he kept his appearance secret. He was a beast.
They tell her to look at him when he is asleep and slay
him. After sex one night, when Eros had fallen asleep,
Psyche lit a lamp, prepared to plunge a dagger into him,
but she found him ravishingly beautiful when she saw
him; and accidentally she pricked herself with one of
his arrows, falling so madly in love that she started to
kiss him. Accidentally, a drop of burning oil fell on him
and awakened him. He flew away.

Revenge

Psyche then sought revenge on her sisters. She visited
each and told them what had happened, convincing
them that it was one of them whom Eros truly loved.
Each went to the mountain to offer herself to her lover
by jumping naively off a cliff to her death. This jumping into the wind to one's death is a mythical motif
and implies the gathering of botanical pharmaceuticals
as the agent for the rapture to the otherworld. The
classic account occurs in Plato's *Phaedrus*: the maiden
Orithyia—Oreithyia—was abducted by the wind from
her sisters while gathering pharmaceutical herbs. Here
it is humorous to imagine the jealous sisters stupidly
throwing themselves off a cliff to what they expect will
be a paradise with their lover. Thematically, however,
it is significant that Psyche was first separated from her
sisters and now is being divested of her sisterhood.

Psyche then went in search of Eros. Both Demeter—Ceres—and Hera—Juno—refused to help and
directed her to Aphrodite. The goddess imposed a series

of tasks. These are the equivalent of the heroic labors of the male hero and involve the motif of the metaphoric entheogen that was the object of the quest.

Unlike the male hero,

Unlike male heroes who conquer nature, Psyche performs impossible tasks by cooperating with Nature, which performs the tasks for her.

however, who conquers some force of nature, Psyche performs the impossible tasks by letting nature perform them for her. For example, she manages to sort a huge pile of seeds by letting ants do it for her. She gathers bits of Golden Fleece from a herd of vicious rams following the advice of a river to wait until they rest in the noonday sun and pick whatever has stuck to the branches and bark of the trees. The advice obviously involves the motif of the Golden Ram as a botanical metaphor, and was probably recognized as such by the novel's original audience. Next, with the help of an eagle, she fetches water flowing from a cleft, impossible to reach and guarded by serpents. None of these count, as far as Aphrodite is concerned, since she didn't do them by herself.

Netherworld

The fourth task was to enter the netherworld and bring back from Persephone a box with stunning beauty in it, to restore the harm that Psyche has caused to the divine appearance of the goddess. Psyche, however, opened the box from curiosity, but saw no beauty in it, only infernal sleep—*narcosis*. Eros found her, woke her, and put the sleep back in its box. Then they petitioned the gods to allow them to marry. Psyche was given a drink of ambrosia, making her immortal and a permanent resident in the empyreal realm.

**Psyche revived by Cupid's Kiss
by Antonio Canova**

Psyche gave birth to a daughter named Voluptas—Greek *Hedonë*. The words are cognate with 'voluptuous' and 'hedonism.' The tale heralds the dawn of a new sexuality, replacing the promiscuous physical coupling of Aphrodite and her lovers with the emotional bond of love.

One can note the transition from the sisterhood to the single female, the duality of the lover as bestial or beautiful, and the acceptance of female sexual pleasure. The theme of visibility or invisibility encodes the mystery of the spirit's consent to reside in flesh. Psyche's beauty, moreover, is superior to that of her mother-in-law, in that she has donned the beauty of Death from the narcotic box of Persephone. Aphrodite's relation to death comes only through her union with Ares (Mars), the god of war, the probable father of Eros. The slaughter of battle thematically involves the rape of the captive women. This is not love between equals, but pure sexual exploitation.

A terra cotta votive plaque from southern Italy contrasts the two ages of sexuality. The chariot of Aphrodite with Hermes represents the erotic physicality of the sex goddess and her stone pillar. Their child will be the Hermaphrodite, who we have seen was responsible for the loveless hypersexuality of nymphomania and satyriasis. Eros and Psyche pull the chariot, holding the cock of Persephone and the unguent vial retrieved from the realm of death. The plaque comes from a cave sanctuary of Persephone at Locri, where the netherworld goddess

was seen as the patroness of marriage. Since the depiction is a votive plaque, it encodes some mystery. Thousands of these plaques were carefully buried in the sanctuary. The numerous depictions of Psyche tormented by
the flaming torches of Eros elevate the simple fairytale
to the rank of theology, implying the yearning of the
soul to embrace the flesh, redeemed with its beloved to
the empyreal realm through a drink of the divine elixir.

   This divine elixir, infused with and derived from
the entheogen, thus permeates the entire mythos with
which Western civilization is familiar – whether expressed through the triple nature of the heroine or the
dual nature of the hero.

Afterword

Never-Ending Path

The 12th Century scholar Maimonides wrote a book called *Guide for the Perplexed*. He was a Jewish mystic and philosopher, living in the Iberian Peninsula during the Golden Age, when it was under Moorish control. Although intended as instruction, the book was apt to leave its reader with knowledge, but still perplexed. Its teachings were offered only as hints, since what it taught was so sensitive that it was not supposed to be expressed, except as misdirection, and even so, it was often prohibited to read or study it.

The final statement of the subject is just the beginning. The reader is invited to follow our suggestions, selecting to pursue whatever seems most enticing. Myth is not a closed and finished subject, but the more you learn, the more it beckons you onward: to seek its meaning and reflections in religion, anthropology, literature, art, history, philosophy—and most intriguing, not only in the past, but ultimately still here, hidden within yourself.

The path keeps going, and whenever you reach a destination, there always seems to be something more to explore, just a little bit further along the way.

BIBLIOGRAPHY

Adittapariyaya Sutta, in Rahula, Walpola, *What the Buddha Taught: Revised and Expanded Edition with Texts from Suttas and Dhammapada* (Grove Press, 1974)

Aeschylus, *Prometheus Bound*, in Vellacott, Philip, *Prometheus Bound and Other Plays* (Penguin, 1961)

Apocryphon of John, in Davies, Stevan L., *The Secret Book of John* (Skylight Paths, 2005)

The Bible, King James Version (American Bible Society, 1980)

Blake, William, *The Marriage of Heaven and Hell*, in Phillips, Michael, *The Marriage of Heaven and Hell* (Bodleian Library, 2011)

Bushman, Richard L., *Joseph Smith: Rough Stone Rolling* (Vintage, 2007)

Campbell, Joseph, *The Hero's Journey* (New World Library, 2003)

Carrera, Juan García, *La Otra Vida de María Sabina* (Universidad Autonoma del Estado de Mexico, 2000)

Carroll, Lewis, *Alice's Adventures in Wonderland* (Dover, 1993)

Carroll, Lewis, *Through the Looking Glass and What Alice Found There* (Dover, 1999)

Doolittle, Hilda, *Tribute to Freud* (New Directions, 2009)

Eliade, Mircea, *Shamanism: Archaic Techniques of Ecstasy* (Princeton University Press, 2004).

Euripedes, *Helen* (Cambridge University Press, 2008)

Euripides, *Herakles* (Oxford University Press, 2001)

Fielding, Henry, *The Life and Death of Tom Thumb the Great* (Gale ECCO, 2012)

Forte, Robert, *Entheogens and the Future of Religion* (Park Street Press, 2012)

Frazer, George, *The Golden Bough* (Konecky & Konecky, 2010)

Freud, Sigmund, *The Medusa's Head*, in Young-Bruehl, Elisabeth, *Freud on Women* (Norton, 1992)

Graves, Robert, *Food for Centaurs* (Doubleday, 1960)

Graves, Robert, *Greek Myths* (Viking, 2011)

Graves, Robert, *I, Claudius* (Random House, 1961).

Grof, Stanislav, *The Potential of Entheogens as Catalysts of Spiritual Development*, in Marley, Greg A., *Chanterelle Dreams, Amanita Nightmares* (Chelsea Green, 2010)

Harner, Michael, *The Way of the Shaman* (HarperOne, 1990)

Harrison, Jane Ellen, *Prolegomena to the Study of Greek Religion* (Forgotten Books, 2012)

Herrick, Robert, *Hesperides* (Nabu Press, 2011)

Hoffman, Albert, *LSD: My Problem Child* (MAPS, 2005)

Huxley, Aldous, *The Doors of Perception and Heaven and Hell* (Perennial Library, 1970)

James, William, *Varieties of Religious Experience* (Megalodon, 2008)

Jung, C.G., *The Personification of the Opposites*, in Schwartz-Salant, Nathan, *Jung on Alchemy* (Princeton University Press, 1995)

Jung, C.G., *Psychology and Religion* (Yale University Press, 1960)

Kurtz, John and Boardman, Donna C., *Greek Burial Customs* (Cornell University Press, 1971)

Lee, John D., *Mormonism Unveiled* (Fierra Blanca, 2001)

Levenda, Peter, *The Secret Temple* (Continuum, 2009)

Lewis, C.S., *Voyage of the Dawn Treader* (Macmillan, 1970)

Maimonides, *Guide of the Perplexed* (University of Chicago Press, 1974)

Needham, Rodney, *Circumstantial Deliveries* (University of California Press, 1982)

Ovid, *Metamorphoses* (Penguin, 2004)

Plato, *Phaedrus* (Penguin, 2005)

Puharich, Andrija, *The Sacred Mushroom: Key to the Door of Eternity* (Doubleday, 1959)

Rigoglioso, Marguerite, *The Cult of Divine Birth in Ancient Greece* (Palgrave Macmillan, 2011)

Rig Veda (Penguin, 2005)

Shanon, Benny, *The Antipodes of the Mind: Charting the Phenomenon of the Ayahuasca Experience* (Oxford University Press, 2003)

Smith, Huston, *Tales of Wonder: Adventures Chasing the Divine* (Harper-One, 2009)

Sophocles, *Ajax* (Hackett, 2007)

Stephens, John Lloyd, *Incidents of Travel in Central America* (Dover, 1969)

Swift, Jonathan, *Gulliver's Travels* (Dover, 1996)

Wasson, R. Gordon, and Wasson, Valentina Pavlovna, *Mushrooms, Russia, and History* (Pantheon, 1957)

Wasson, R. Gordon, *Soma: Divine Mushroom of Immortality* (Harcourt Brace Jovanovich, 1972)

Wasson, R. Gordon, *The Wondrous Mushroom: Mycolatry in Mesoamerica* (McGraw-Hill, 1980)

fURTHER ReADINC

Ruck, R. Gordon Wasson, and Albert Hofmann, *The Road to Eleusis: Unveiling the Secret of the Mysteries* (1978, 1998, 2008)

Ruck, R. Gordon Wasson, Stella Kramrisch, and Jonathan Ott, *Persephone's Quest: Entheogens and the Origins of Religion* (Yale, 1986)

Ruck and Danny (Blaise) Staples, *The World of Classical Myth: Gods and Goddesses, Heroines and Heroes* (Carolina Academic Press, 1994)

Ruck, Blaise Staples, and Clark Heinrich, *The Apples of Apollo: Pagan and Christian Mysteries of the Eucharist* (Carolina Academic Press, 2000)

Ruck, *Sacred Mushrooms of the Goddess: Secrets of Eleusis* (Ronin, 2006)

Ruck, Staples, Hoffman, and José Alfredo González Celdrán, *The Hidden World: Survival of Pagan Shamanic Themes in European Fairytales* (Carolina Academic Press, 2007)

Ruck, Brian Akers, Juan Francisco Ruiz, and Alan Piper, "A Prehistoric Mural in Spain Depicting Neurotropic *Psilocybe* Mushrooms?": 1-8 in *Economic Botany*, vol. 20, no. 10, 2011

Ruck, Hoffman, and González Celdrán, *Mushrooms, Myth & Mithras: The Drug Cult that Civilized Europe* (City Lights Books, 2011)

Ruck and Hoffman, *The Effluents of Deity: Alchemy and Psychoactive Sacraments in Medieval and Renaissance Art* (Carolina Academic Press, 2012)

Ruck, and Robert Larner, "Virgil's Edible Tables," in John Rush, *Entheogens and the Development of Culture: An Anthology and Neurobiology of Ecstatic Experience* (North Atlantic Books, 2013)

Ruck, "Democracy and the Dionysian Agenda," in John Rush, *Entheogens and the Development of Culture: An Anthology and Neurobiology of Ecstatic Experience* (North Atlantic Books, 2013)

Legal Status

The Controlled Substances Act (CSA) regulates manufacture, importation, possession, use, and distribution of substances deemed harmful or liable for potential abuse, on a five-degree scale or 'Schedule'.

In 1993, the United States Congress passed the Religious Freedom Restoration Act (RFRA) recognizing that the religious freedom of certain pre-conquest indigenous peoples is limited by criminalizing of psychoactive plants used as a sacrament in their rituals and has particular relevance to the Native American Church (NAC) and its peyote sacrament. To qualify for this exemption, a candidate must demonstrate ethnic purity.

In 2006, the United States Supreme Court reversed the decision of the lower court of New Mexico which restricted the access of the *Centro Espirita Beneficente União do Vegetal* (UDV Church) to *hoasca* tea or *ayahuasca*—a psychoactive sacrament combining two

Prohibition Poster

Amazonian plants, usually *Banisteriopsis caapi* and *Psychotria viridis*. The Church of *Santo Daime* has the same sacrament so supported the UDV in its appeal.

The Controlled Substances Act has proven largely unenforceable and stimulated the growth of organized crime—much as Prohibition did.

About the Authors

Carl A. P. Ruck

Professor of Classics at Boston University, Dr. Carl A. P. Ruck is an authority on the ecstatic rituals of the god Dionysus. In *Persephone's Quest: Entheogens and the Origins of Religion*, he proclaimed the centrality of psychoactive sacraments at the very beginnings of religion, employing the neologism "entheogen" to free the topic from the pejorative connotations for words like drug or hallucinogen. Dr. Ruck is author of:

Sacred Mushrooms of the Goddess
Secrets of Eleusis

Mushrooms, Myth, and Mithras
The Drug Cult that Civilized Europe

The World of Classical Myth
Gods and Goddesses, Heroines and Heroes

The Apples of Apollo
Pagan and Christian Mysteries of the Eucharist

The Hidden World
Survival of Pagan Shamanic Themes in European Fairytales

Mark A. Hoffman

Mark Hoffman is an entheogen scholar and Editor of *Entheos: Journal of Psychedelic Spirituality*. He has been a contributor and collaborated on several projects with Dr. Ruck, including *The Hidden World* and *Mushrooms, Myth, and Mithras*.

9 781579 511418